Acing

Civil Procedure

Second Edition

**A Checklist Approach to
Solving Procedural Problems**

A. Benjamin Spencer

Associate Professor of Law

*Washington & Lee University
School of Law*

Series Editor

A. Benjamin Spencer

THOMSON

™

WEST

Mat #40743587

© West, a Thomson business, 2005
© 2008 Thomson/West
610 Opperman Drive
St. Paul, MN 55123
1–800–313–9378

Printed in the United States of America

ISBN: 978–0–314–19400–8

 TEXT IS PRINTED ON 10% POST CONSUMER RECYCLED PAPER

For Marlette, Isabella, Mya, James and Mary Alice

*

About the Author

A. BENJAMIN SPENCER is an Associate Professor of Law at Washington & Lee University School of Law. He is a graduate of Morehouse College, The London School of Economics, and Harvard Law School, where he was an Articles Editor of the *Harvard Law Review*. After law school, Professor Spencer served a one-year clerkship with Judge Judith W. Rogers of the U.S. Court of Appeals for the D.C. Circuit. Before becoming a law professor, Professor Spencer worked as a Litigation Associate in a New York-based law firm for two years. He teaches and publishes in the area of civil procedure, with his current research interests focused on federal civil pleading standards.

*

Preface

This book was written to help the large number of students who emerge every year from their civil procedure courses dazed and confused. Civil procedure for many is the most confounding of subjects, dealing with technical arcana that beginning law students have a difficult time getting their minds around. Civil procedure does not have to be so difficult and indeed can be quite interesting to study. After teaching my own students the topic, I learned early on that they would benefit greatly from a useful organizing tool that brought all of the material for each subject together, not only in a way that would facilitate understanding, but also in a way that could be used to solve the problems they would face in working through classroom hypotheticals or examination questions. So I began developing checklists for their benefit that I presented to my students at the end of each unit. I found the students not only to be extremely grateful for this information, but it was universally reported to me that these checklists greatly enhanced their understanding of the material and gave them a method for attacking procedural problems that they otherwise might have had difficulty developing on their own.

It is with the goal of sharing this useful tool with students beyond those in my own classes that I offer this book. I hope that readers find these checklists to be as useful as my students have found them to be.

*

Table of Contents

*

Introduction

When I was in law school, most students spent a good deal of time developing an outline for each course—a lengthy (I've seen outlines well over 100 pages in length) and exhaustive document that purports to compile the universe of information presented in a course into an organized, accessible format that would simplify studying and provide a useful source for information during the exam (provided the exam was open-book).

I too engaged in this time-honored practice, using a collection of previously-developed outlines and my own class notes to form my own version of an outline for each course. Beyond its usefulness as a reference tool during my exams, I found the process of drafting outlines useful in forcing me to review my notes and other materials in a more meaningful way than simply re-reading those materials would have demanded.

Unfortunately, my outlines never were able to provide me with anything more than a restatement of various principles of law or doctrine organized by topic; it remained for me to take those doctrines and apply them to the fact patterns presented in my exams. That process of applying legal principles to facts is a large part of what law school, law school exams, and lawyering are all about; knowing the relevant law is only half (oftentimes less than half) of the battle. So why were I and my fellow students devoting all of this time and energy into developing these miniature tomes on the law of Contracts, Torts, Civil Procedure, etc., and not putting more energy into developing a tool that could help guide our legal analysis of problems presented on exams?

In addition to an outline, there was another document that some students including myself occasionally developed as an examination aid: the checklist. There was not a single definition for a checklist or a consistent approach to drafting one. But at bottom, a checklist was meant to present in a sparse and simplified way the basics about a topic that one wanted to be sure to remember to discuss or evaluate in the course of one's examination answer. Some checklists were simply bullet points of elements or rules under larger topical headings. Others were more involved in linking various concepts together in a logical pattern that facilitated the analysis of legal problems. Regardless of the format, I never developed or came across a checklist for any of my courses that made much of a contribution beyond being a condensed form of the lengthier outline prepared for the course.

Since I started teaching as a law professor, I have given the checklist a second look. Properly conceived and crafted, I have come to believe that checklists can fulfill the role of providing a tool that truly aids students in their effort to analyze legal problems in their courses. I define a useful checklist as follows: A document that presents the series of questions that must be asked and answered, in sequence, in order to resolve a legal issue that is presented.

There is a general structure to legal analysis that involves identifying the issue, articulating the applicable legal rules and principles, applying those principles to a given set of facts, and then arriving at and stating a conclusion.[1] While this structure provides a sound overarching approach to tackling legal problems, the process of identifying the relevant legal principle and then applying it to the situation is typically more involved than this general model suggests. The process of arriving at the right rule and application of that rule is somewhat akin to the thought process

---

1. This method of analysis is referred to by many as the I–R–A–C method, with the letters standing for Issue, Rule, Application (or Analysis), and Conclusion.

illustrated by decision trees, where the way in which an initial question is answered determines which of several alternative paths one follows in order to get to the next appropriate question.

For example, if a person is trying to decide whether she can proceed to drive through an intersection with a traffic signal, the first question she might ask is, "Is the signal green?" If the answer is no, then the answer to the original question is no, she cannot proceed. But if the answer is yes, then the driver is led to another question: "Are there any cars passing through the intersection via the cross street?" If the answer to this question is yes, then the answer to the original question is no, the driver should not proceed. However, a "no" answer might lead the driver to yet another question: "Are there any pedestrians crossing the street I am on?" Again, an affirmative answer requires a negative response to the initial question regarding proceeding through the intersection. If there are no pedestrians crossing the street, then the driver may at last conclude that she may drive through the intersection.[2]

In the above example, there are a collection of rules or principles that govern whether one can go through an intersection: the indications being given by any regulatory signals or signs, the presence of any obstructions, the existence of any threats to safe passage, and the threat to others that one's passage may pose. Identifying these rules and then applying them to the situation requires an analytical structure that organizes these rules into a series of relevant inquiries that will efficiently channel the thought process in order to arrive at a decision or finding.

Thus, a checklist as I have defined it is the document that organizes a collection of rules into a decision tree of sorts by identifying all of the relevant questions that one must ask and answer in order to completely analyze a question. The checklist for

---

2. Or the driver could continue with another inquiry: "Are there any dangerous objects that I would have to drive over like nails or glass in my path?" Answering no would allow the driver to move forward, while a yes answer would counsel hesitation. There may be additional questions one could pose in this situation.

our intersection example above might look something like the
following:

PASSAGE THROUGH INTERSECTIONS
WITH TRAFFIC SIGNALS

A. Is the traffic signal displaying green?

    1. If no, then you may not proceed through the intersection.[3]

    2. If yes, proceed to the next question.

B. Is there traffic crossing the intersection via the cross street?

    1. If yes, then you may not proceed through the intersection.

    2. If no, proceed to the next question.

C. Are there pedestrians obstructing safe passage?

    1. If yes, then you may not proceed through the intersection.

    2. If no, proceed to the next question.

**D. Are there any dangerous objects in the road that should be
avoided?**

    1. If yes, then you may not proceed through the intersection.

    2. If no, then you may proceed through the intersection.

Not only does the checklist effectively lead the driver to the correct
decision, it ensures that no important questions are forgotten in the
analysis.

Checklists for law school course topics serve the same
function. At the end of a course, students have a multitude of rules
and principles at their disposal and need a means of tidily organiz-

---

3. My wife asked, "What should I do if the   intersection (although that clearly is not the
signal is yellow?" I will assume that a yellow   case for everyone!).
signal would also suggest stopping at the

ing them in a way that will facilitate analysis of problems on the exam and will make certain that important rules or exceptions are not overlooked in the process.

The purpose of this book is to present law students with a comprehensive set of checklists pertaining to each of the topics typically covered in first-year federal civil procedure courses. The checklists are meant to provide students with a tool that facilitates their analysis of procedural problems. Each chapter will focus on a different topic, first presenting a brief review of the subject followed by the checklist for the subject. After the checklist has been presented, hypothetical problems will be analyzed to illustrate how the checklists can be used to resolve such problems. Each chapter will conclude with a section entitled "Points to Remember" to recapitulate key points that students need to remember when answering exam questions. A concluding chapter provides some final thoughts on preparing for and taking exams generally. At the end of the book there is an Appendix that presents condensed one- or two-page "mini-checklists" for each topic. Students may find these useful during the time crunch of an exam when they need quick access to the full range of major concepts that are pertinent to an issue.

Students should use this book to assist themselves in developing their own analytical process for resolving the questions they will face on their examinations. The steps outlined in the checklists presented here can provide students with a map for how they should proceed when evaluating any given legal issue. Funneling one's analysis through the checklist will also improve the chances that one's answer will fully display a reasoned analysis while also arriving at a sound conclusion. But these checklists can only be used effectively by those who possess a thorough understanding of the substantive material.

This book is not a hornbook and does not attempt to explain civil procedure doctrines in any great detail; rather, it merely seeks to organize doctrine into a dynamic tool that students can use to apply legal principles to fact patterns they will face on exams. Students should thus use these checklists in conjunction with other substantive material in order best to prepare for their exams. That being said, use of these checklists should enhance the ability of the student to write reasoned and sound responses to examination questions. Further, these checklists should be helpful in putting the course material in perspective and providing a clearer picture of how the concepts students are learning should be integrated into a legal analysis. Finally, students should make sure to modify these checklists according to the areas of emphasis and coverage of their professors in their respective classes.

CHAPTER 1

Personal Jurisdiction

Personal jurisdiction, as the topic is commonly labeled,[1] pertains to the authority of a court to render a decision that will bind the parties before it. The general rule in federal courts is that jurisdiction over the defendant is proper where the defendant could be subjected to the jurisdiction of courts of the state where the federal district court is located.[2] This means that the rules and legal doctrines governing personal jurisdiction in a state court will generally be the same principles that determine personal jurisdiction in the federal courts.

PERSONAL JURISDICTION REVIEW

Personal jurisdiction analysis involves two main steps: (1) a determination of whether the state's long-arm statute confers jurisdic-

---

1. A more appropriate term might be "territorial jurisdiction," which would include *in rem* and *quasi in rem* assertions of jurisdiction, as well as *in personam* jurisdiction. Nonetheless, the phrase "personal jurisdiction" has come to serve as the moniker for the topic covering all three types of territorial jurisdiction.

2. FED. R. CIV. P. 4(k)(1)(A). Rule 4 also provides alternative bases for establishing personal jurisdiction in federal courts, such as permitting jurisdiction over those defendants located within 100 miles of the courthouse and made party to the action under Rules 14 or 19 (the "100–mile Bulge Rule" of Rule 4(k)(1)(B)) or permitting personal jurisdiction on the basis of special service provisions found in certain federal statutes where the action arises under such a statute (Rule 4(k)(1)(C)). When the defendant is not subject to personal jurisdiction in *any* state (a possibility largely for non-U.S. defendants), Rule 4(k)(2) provides that service of process can establish personal jurisdiction—for federal question claims only—over such defendants if jurisdiction is consistent with the U.S. Constitution. These alternatives are integrated into the checklist below.

tion and (2) an analysis of whether the federal constitution—specifically the Due Process Clause of the Fourteenth Amendment—permits the particular exercise of personal jurisdiction in the case at hand. Analyzing the long-arm statute usually is not the more difficult task; rather, it is the constitutional analysis that will consume the bulk of one's energy in this process. However, students should be aware of the two general types of long-arm statutes that exist. One type of long-arm statute simply authorizes jurisdiction to the extent it is permitted under the federal constitution. This variant, exemplified by the long-arm statutes in California and Rhode Island, eschews any state-based constraint on jurisdiction and relies solely on the scope of jurisdiction allowable under the Due Process Clause. Thus, no separate analysis as to whether the long-arm statute itself permits jurisdiction is necessary where such a statute is at issue.

The other type of long-arm statute takes the opposite approach and specifically articulates the factual circumstances under which state courts will be permitted to exercise jurisdiction. This type of long-arm statute is referred to as an *enumerated act* statute. When an enumerated act statute applies, one must first determine whether the facts presented qualify for jurisdiction under the statute and then consider whether the constitution permits such an exercise of jurisdiction.[3]

Constitutional personal jurisdiction analysis is rooted in the case of **International Shoe Co. v. Washington**,[4] which established the fundamental test for whether assertions of personal jurisdiction are consistent with the Due Process Clause of the Fourteenth Amendment of the U.S. Constitution: jurisdiction may be exercised if the defendant has "certain minimum contacts with [the forum] such that the maintenance of the suit does not offend 'traditional notions of fair play and substantial justice.' "[5] This standard supplanted in

---

3. In reality, many states have interpreted their enumerated act statutes to extend jurisdiction to the constitutional limit, rendering them effectively no different in application from the broad California-style long-arm statutes. Thus, in practice one should consult the forum state's interpretation of its long-arm statute before applying it to a particular set of facts.

4. 326 U.S. 310 (1945).

5. *Id.* at 318 (citation omitted).

large part the previous standard of territoriality established by the Supreme Court in *Pennoyer v. Neff*.[6] The Supreme Court has expounded upon the *International Shoe* standard and has provided several examples of its application over the years, resulting in some guidance on how this standard is to be applied in various contexts. However, this guidance has not presented clear black-and-white rules; rather, what has emerged are standards that guide one's analysis but ultimately result in less predictability in jurisdictional outcomes than the Supreme Court has indicated it wishes to promote.

In articulating the minimum contacts standard, the Court in *International Shoe* indicated that contacts should be evaluated with reference to whether they are "continuous and systematic" versus "single or isolated" and with respect to whether they "give rise to the liabilities sued on" or are "unconnected" with the cause of action.[7] These attributes can be combined to create four categories of contacts that can be used to keep track of the Court's position as to whether contacts of a particular sort will or will not constitute minimum contacts equaling fair play and substantial justice.

Fact patterns falling within the first category—where contacts are systematic and continuous and give rise to the claim—will always enjoy jurisdiction according to the Court.[8] The second category, involving systematic and continuous contacts that are unrelated to the cause of action, has come to represent the area of general jurisdiction; jurisdiction is appropriate for this category of cases if the systematic and continuous contacts can be described as "substantial."[9] Although the Court has not given clear guidance

---

6. 95 U.S. 714, 722 (1877) (establishing that "every State possesses exclusive jurisdiction and sovereignty over persons and property within its territory" but that "no State can exercise direct jurisdiction and authority over persons or property without its territory").

7. *Int'l Shoe*, 326 U.S. at 317.

8. *See id.* ("'Presence' in the state in this sense has never been doubted when the activities of the corporation there have not only been continuous and systematic, but also give rise to the liabilities sued on, even though no consent to be sued or authorization to an agent to accept service of process has been given.").

9. *Id.* at 318 ("[T]here have been instances in which the continuous corporate operations within a state were thought so substantial and of such a nature as to justify suit

regarding what facts would qualify as indicating substantial contacts, such contacts appear to be those approaching the conduct of extensive corporate operations, management, and/or administrative activity within a state.[10] The third category involves isolated and sporadic contacts giving rise to the cause of action. Cases falling within this category are referred to as specific jurisdiction cases. Most of the court's personal jurisdiction jurisprudence has concentrated on this area. Jurisdiction is appropriate for this category of cases if the defendant can be said to have purposefully availed itself of the forum state and if the assertion of jurisdiction would be reasonable.[11] The final category identified by the Court in *International Shoe* consists of those cases involving isolated but unrelated contacts. For this category of cases the *International Shoe* Court declared there could be no personal jurisdiction based on such contacts.[12] These four categories can be arrayed in a matrix as follows:

FOUR-POSITION PERSONAL JURISDICTION MATRIX
from *International Shoe*

NATURE OF CONTACTS	Related	Unrelated
Continuous & Systematic	Jurisdiction	General jurisdiction if contacts are "substantial"
Isolated & Sporadic	Specific jurisdiction if purposeful availment and reasonableness requirements satisfied	No Jurisdiction

against it on causes of action arising from dealings entirely distinct from those activities."). *See also* Helicopteros v. Hall, 466 U.S. 408 (1984); Perkins v. Benguet, 342 U.S. 437 (1952).

10. *Perkins,* 342 U.S. at 447–48.

11. *See* Burger King Corporation v. Rudzewicz, 471 U.S. 462 (1985).

12. *See Int'l Shoe,* 326 U.S. at 317 ("[T]he casual presence of the corporate agent or even his conduct of single or isolated items of activities in a state in the corporation's behalf are not enough to subject it to suit on causes of action unconnected with the activities there.").

Under the specific jurisdiction analysis, the Court imposes a purposeful availment requirement as the standard by which courts determine whether the minimum contacts prong of the *International Shoe* test is satisfied. Purposeful availment requires that there be "some act by which the defendant purposefully avails itself of the privilege of conducting activities within the forum state, thus invoking the benefits and protections of its laws."[13] This requirement is thought to ensure that defendants will be on clear notice regarding where their conduct will and will not subject them to jurisdiction.[14]

Although the Court is interested in ensuring that defendants have notice of where they will be subject to personal jurisdiction, merely being able to foresee that one's actions will cause injury in the forum is not sufficient to establish personal jurisdiction.[15] However, where a defendant engages in intentional wrongful conduct that has effects within a state, the Court has held such conduct to be a sufficient basis for personal jurisdiction in that state.[16] Entering into a contract with a forum resident can also constitute purposeful availment under the so-called contracts-plus analysis, where one considers the place of negotiation, execution, and performance of the contract to determine whether these factors support a finding of purposeful availment of the forum.[17] Finally, it should be noted that purposeful availment cannot exist on the basis of the unilateral actions of the plaintiff or third parties; rather, jurisdiction must be based on actions of the defendant.[18]

Once it is determined that minimum contacts exist, one still must determine whether the assertion of personal jurisdiction would be reasonable.[19] The reasonableness requirement for specific

---

13. Hanson v. Denckla, 357 U.S. 235, 253 (1958).

14. *See* World–Wide Volkswagen Corp. v. Woodson, 444 U.S. 286 (1980).

15. *See id.* at 295–96.

16. Calder v. Jones, 465 U.S. 783 (1984).

17. Burger King v. Rudzewicz, 471 U.S. 462

(1985); McGee v. Int'l Life Ins. Co., 355 U.S. 220 (1957).

18. Hanson v. Denckla, 357 U.S. 235 (1958).

19. The defendant carries the burden of demonstrating that the assertion of personal jurisdiction would be unreasonable. *See Burger King*, 471 U.S. at 477 ("[W]here a

jurisdiction cases is used to determine whether a particular assertion of jurisdiction would comport with fair play and substantial
justice, the other part of the *International Shoe* test. A reasonableness
review involves a five-factor analysis evaluating (1) the burden on
the defendant, (2) the forum State's interest in adjudicating the
dispute, (3) the plaintiff's interest in obtaining convenient and
effective relief, (4) the interstate judicial system's interest in obtaining the most efficient resolution of controversies, and (5) the shared
interest of the several States in furthering fundamental substantive
social policies.[20] The first three factors have proven to be the most
significant, with the Court not articulating a clear vision of how
factors four and five are to be evaluated.[21]

The failure to find minimum contacts generally should end
the inquiry, resulting in a finding that personal jurisdiction would
not be proper without regard to whether an assertion of jurisdiction would be reasonable. However, the Court has not conclusively
resolved how to balance the two prongs of the *International Shoe* test,
with Justice O'Connor's plurality opinion in ***Asahi Metal v. Superior
Court***[22] proceeding with a reasonableness analysis notwithstanding
its conclusion that minimum contacts were lacking.[23] Indeed,
Justice Brennan has suggested that the *International Shoe* test should
be treated as a sliding scale, with a more substantial showing of
minimum contacts making up for a lesser showing for the reasonableness prong, and vice versa; thus, under Justice Brennan's view,
where minimum contacts are thin, a strong showing of reasonableness can still support the assertion of personal jurisdiction.[24]

The Court has spoken on the propriety of personal jurisdiction in several specific contexts. When an individual (rather than

---

defendant who purposefully has directed his
activities at forum residents seeks to defeat
jurisdiction, he must present a compelling
case that the presence of some other considerations would render jurisdiction
unreasonable.").

20. *Id.*

21. See *Asahi Metal v. Superior Court*, 480
U.S. 102 (1987), for an application of the five
factors by the Court.

22. 480 U.S. 102 (1987).

23. *See id.* at 113.

24. *Burger King*, 471 U.S at 477 ("[Fair play]
considerations sometimes serve to establish
the reasonableness of jurisdiction upon a
lesser showing of minimum contacts than
would otherwise be required.").

corporate) defendant is served with process in a state, such in-state service suffices to establish the constitutionality of personal jurisdiction, without reference to whether such an assertion would be reasonable.[25] However, when the defendant's in-state presence is procured by fraud, most courts would likely find that jurisdiction has not properly been secured and thus any ensuing judgment would be void for want of jurisdiction.[26] As alluded to earlier, in the intentional torts context, the Court has held that intentionally targeting wrongful conduct towards a forum resident will support an assertion of jurisdiction in the victim's state of residence if they suffer harm there.[27] This is known as the *Calder* "effects" test, named for the case in which the test was developed, **Calder v. Jones**.[28] For cases involving contacts mediated through the so-called "stream of commerce," the Court has split over the appropriate mode of analysis. Justice O'Connor's view in **Asahi Metal v. Superior Court**[29] was that the mere placement of a product into the stream of commerce is insufficient to establish minimum contacts; rather, the party must intend to serve the forum state when it participates in the stream of commerce.[30] Justice Brennan on the other hand felt that placing a product into the stream of commerce with the awareness that it would be marketed in the forum state sufficed to establish minimum contacts with that state.[31] No majority formed on the Court in support of either view, and thus lower courts have been left to select the approach that they prefer, leaning towards the approach endorsed by Justice O'Connor.

---

25. Burnham v. Superior Court, 495 U.S. 604, 619 (1990). Justice Brennan believed that a reasonableness analysis was necessary even when jurisdiction is based on in-state service but lower courts have rejected this position. *See id.* at 629 (Brennan, J., concurring) ("I would undertake an independent inquiry into the . . . fairness of the prevailing in-state service rule."). Although Justice Scalia's opinion in *Burnham* endorsing in-state service as a basis for jurisdiction without regard to reasonableness was only a plurality opinion, his view has prevailed as the accepted justification for the in-state service rule.

26. Wyman v. Newhouse, 93 F.2d 313 (2d Cir. 1937).

27. Calder v. Jones, 465 U.S. 783 (1984). Note that a separate analysis of the reasonableness prong of the *International Shoe* test is unnecessary if the *Calder* "effects" test is satisfied.

28. *Id.*

29. 480 U.S. 102 (1987).

30. *See Asahi*, 480 U.S. at 112.

31. *See id.* at 117.

The Supreme Court has not spoken on the issue of when personal jurisdiction can be based on Internet contacts. Among the lower courts, the framework established by a Pennsylvania district court in *Zippo Manufacturing Co. v. Zippo Dot Com, Inc.*[32]—which classifies websites as passive, active, or interactive, with jurisdiction being appropriate where the website is active but reserving judgment on interactive sites—has been influential in shaping the approach of many district and circuit courts.[33] Today, although Zippo's influence persists, courts tend to focus on whether contacts mediated through the Internet are specifically directed to the forum state before permitting the contacts to serve as the basis for personal jurisdiction there.[34]

Several exceptions to the requirements of traditional jurisdictional analysis exist. If a party consents to jurisdiction, such as in a forum selection clause[35] or a state domestication statute,[36] jurisdiction is constitutional. Similarly, jurisdiction can be imposed on defendants where they have waived any challenge to jurisdiction, which can occur if they fail to object to personal jurisdiction in their initial response to the complaint.[37] Jurisdiction is also constitutional

---

32. 952 F. Supp. 1119 (W.D. Pa. 1997).

33. *See, e.g.*, Toys "R" Us, Inc. v. Step Two, S.A., 318 F.3d 446, 452 (3d Cir. 2003); Lakin v. Prudential Securities, Inc., 348 F.3d 704, 711 (8th Cir. 2003); ALS Scan Inc. v. Digital Service Consultants, Inc., 293 F.3d 707 (4th Cir. 2002); Cybersell, Inc. v. Cybersell, Inc., 130 F.3d 414, 418–19 (9th Cir. 1997). A contrary standard was established prior to *Zippo* in *Inset Systems v. Instruction Set, Inc.*, 937 F. Supp. 161 (D. Conn. 1996), which held that the presence of a website advertising one's product is sufficient to establish purposeful availment in every state where the website is available. This position was not generally adopted by other courts.

34. *See, e.g.*, Good v. Fuji Fire & Marine Ins. Co., 2008 WL 822453, at *3 (10th Cir. Mar. 27, 2008) ("The extent to which jurisdiction can be established by an Internet presence, however, depends on the degree to which the web site is used to conduct or solicit business within the forum."); McBee v. Delica Co., 417 F.3d 107, 124 (1st Cir. 2005) ("[T]he mere existence of a website that is visible in a forum and that gives information about a company and its products is not enough, by itself, to subject a defendant to personal jurisdiction in that forum.").

35. *See, e.g.*, Carnival Cruise Lines, Inc. v. Shute, 499 U.S. 585, 594–95 (1991).

36. A state domestication statute is a statute that extracts consent to jurisdiction from companies as a condition of registering to do business within a state. *See, e.g.*, Kane v. New Jersey, 242 U.S. 160 (1916).

37. FED. R. CIV. P. 12(h). The filing of a notice of a removal, something we will review in Chapter 2, does not operate as a waiver of the defendant's right to challenge personal jurisdiction. *See* Morris & Co. v. Skandinavia Ins. Co., 279 U.S. 405, 409 (1929); Silva v. City of Madison, 69 F.3d 1368 (7th Cir. 1995). Defendants who do object to jurisdiction, but

when exercised over forum state citizens[38] or non-resident plaintiffs[39] without reference to the minimum contacts test. Jurisdiction in *in rem* actions—which involve disputes over interests in property[40]—must satisfy the minimum contacts test according to *Shaffer v. Heitner*, but this will generally be the case so typically no real analysis is necessary.[41] *Quasi in rem* actions,[42] however, per *Shaffer*, must be scrutinized under the minimum contacts test of *International Shoe*.[43]

Defendants wishing to challenge the personal jurisdiction of a federal district court may do so either by moving to dismiss for lack of personal jurisdiction under Rule 12(b)(2) or by challenging jurisdiction in their answer, provided the answer serves as their initial response to the complaint.[44] However, if the defendant foregoes any direct challenge to personal jurisdiction and fails to appear at all in an action, he may still collaterally attack[45] a resulting

---

fail to comply with court orders surrounding jurisdictional discovery can be deemed to be estopped from challenging personal jurisdiction. *See* Insurance Corp. of Ireland v. Compagnie des Bauxites de Guinee, 456 U.S. 694 (1982).

38. Milliken v. Meyer, 311 U.S. 457, 463 (1940).

39. Adam v. Saenger, 303 U.S. 59, 67–68 (1938). Plaintiffs bringing an action in a court have selected that forum and thus have consented to or waived any right to challenge the court's jurisdiction over them for any ensuing claims asserted against them within that action.

40. Most states treat a divorce action as an *in rem* proceeding, treating marital status as the property or *res* over which jurisdiction is exercised.

41. *Shaffer*, 433 U.S. at 207–08 ("[W]hen claims to the property itself are the source of the underlying controversy between the plaintiff and the defendant, it would be unusual for the State where the property is located not to have jurisdiction. In such cases, the defendant's claim to property located in the State would normally indicate that he expected to benefit from the State's

protection of his interest.").

42. *Quasi in rem* actions include those actions where property that is not the subject of the action but lies within the jurisdiction of the court is used to provide the plaintiff with a basis for jurisdiction and a resource for the satisfaction of any judgment obtained in the action; this approach is typically used when *in personam* jurisdiction over the defendant in the jurisdiction is not attainable.

43. *Shaffer*, 433 U.S. at 212 ("We therefore conclude that all assertions of state-court jurisdiction must be evaluated according to the standards set forth in *International Shoe* and its progeny.").

44. Again, filing a notice of a removal prior to submitting any other response is not treated as a waiver of the defendant's right to challenge personal jurisdiction. The mechanics of making pre-answer motions and the rules governing their waiver are covered in Chapter 9.

45. A collateral attack is a challenge to a judgment made not on direct appeal but rather in a subsequent proceeding. Such a challenge can take the form of a declaratory action seeking a declaration of the invalidity default judgment on the basis of a lack of personal jurisdiction in the initial action. Because of the possibility that jurisdictional challenges can be waived, when addressing a personal jurisdiction question on an exam it is always worthwhile to make a quick check of whether such waiver has occurred.

 PERSONAL JURISDICTION CHECKLIST

With the above review in mind, the personal jurisdiction checklist is presented below:

A. FEDERAL OR STATE COURT? If the case is in state court, the limits on state court jurisdiction apply. Proceed to Part B of this checklist. If the case is in federal court, Rules 4(k) and 12 must be consulted.

    1. Possible Waiver? Consult Rule 12—FRCP Rule 12 requires defendants to raise any challenge to personal jurisdiction in their initial response or the challenge is waived.[46] Thus, it is critical at this point to determine whether the defendant has waived a personal jurisdiction challenge. If so, personal jurisdiction is appropriate.[47]

    2. Rule 4(k)—does the general rule of 4(k)(1)(A) apply or is there an alternate applicable provision for establishing jurisdiction? If one of the alternate provisions applies, then compliance with 4(k)(1)(A)—which incorporates states' standards of personal jurisdiction—will be unnecessary. Possible options under Rule 4(k) to consider:

        a. **100-Mile Bulge Rule**—is the party one that was joined under Rule 14 or 19 and served within a judicial district

---

of the judgment or can arise as a defense to an action seeking to enforce the judgment in another jurisdiction.

46. Filing a notice of removal prior to submitting any other response does not constitute waiver of a personal jurisdiction challenge.

47. Note that waiver may be a possibility in state court as well, but subject to rules that may vary from that contained in Federal Rule 12.

not more than 100 miles from the place where the summons issued? If so, jurisdiction can be established under Rule 4(k)(1)(B). If not, proceed to the next question.

b. **Federal statutory provision**—is there a federal statute involved here that has its own service provisions, compliance with which would establish personal jurisdiction? If so, jurisdiction can be established under Rule 4(k)(1)(C) by complying with the special service provision. If not, proceed to the next question.

c. **Alien provision**—is this a claim arising under federal law against a person not subject to personal jurisdiction in any state? If so, service will render the defendant subject to personal jurisdiction if it has minimum contacts with the United States (Rule 4(k)(2)). Proceed to the constitutional analysis below in Part C but analyze minimum contacts with reference to the United States as a whole rather than a particular State.

d. **Rule 4(k)(1)(A)**—if none of these alternative provisions of Rule 4(k) apply, you will have to follow Rule 4(k)(1)(A), which requires you to determine whether the defendant could be subjected to the jurisdiction of a court of general jurisdiction in the state in which the district court is located. Refer to the analysis beginning at Part B of this checklist to make this determination.

B. **LONG-ARM STATUTE**—does the state's long-arm statute authorize personal jurisdiction under these facts?

1. **Type of Long-Arm Statute**—what type of long-arm statute does the forum state have?

a. **Rhode Island Model**—authorizes courts to exercise jurisdiction to the constitutional limit. If this type of statute is involved, no further statutory analysis is required and you may proceed to the constitutional analysis beginning at Part C.

b. **Enumerated Act Model**—specifically articulates factual circumstances where courts can exercise personal jurisdiction. If this type of statute is involved, proceed to the next question.

2. **Statutory Analysis**—do the facts presented fall within one of the categories articulated in the long-arm statute?[48]

    a. **Yes.** If the facts fall within the long-arm statute, proceed to the constitutional analysis of Part C.

    b. **No.** If the facts do not fall within the long-arm statute, then personal jurisdiction cannot be exercised over the party. Your analysis ends here.[49]

C. **CONSTITUTIONAL ANALYSIS**—does the assertion of jurisdiction satisfy the requirements of due process?

1. **Traditional Bases for Personal Jurisdiction**—is one of the traditional bases for personal jurisdiction applicable?

    a. **In-state service.** Was the defendant an individual served with process within the state? If so, jurisdiction is proper. *Burnham v. Superior Court*, 495 U.S. 604 (1990). However, where the defendant's in-state presence is procured by fraud, jurisdiction may not be proper. *See, e.g.*, *Wyman v. Newhouse*, 93 F.2d 313 (2d Cir. 1937).

    b. **Voluntary Appearance.** Has the defendant voluntarily appeared and proceeded to defend itself in the action without challenging personal jurisdiction? If so, the court will have personal jurisdiction over the defendant.

2. **Exceptions to Jurisdictional Analysis**—If no traditional basis for personal jurisdiction is present, does an exception to traditional jurisdictional analysis apply?

    a. **Consent.** Did the defendant consent to jurisdiction in the state?

        i. **Forum Selection Clause**—is there a forum selection clause? If so, does it apply to this dispute? *See Carnival*

---

48. Remember, in practice, it is best to refer to the interpretation of the long-arm statute given by the state's highest court to see if the statute is interpreted as extending jurisdiction to the constitutional limit, notwithstanding its status as an enumerated act statute.

49. If you are uncertain of this conclusion, the better practice may be to continue on with your analysis in the event that your conclusion regarding the long-arm statute is incorrect. However, where the facts clearly do not fall within the terms of the long-arm statute, and the statute is not one that has been interpreted to extend to the constitutional limit, you should not waste valuable exam time engaging in a needless constitutional analysis.

Cruise Lines, Inc. v. Shute, 499 U.S. 585 (1991) (holding that forum selection clauses are generally enforceable).

ii. **State Domestication Statute**—is there a state statute exacting consent from the defendant (e.g., through corporate registration; non-resident motorist statute)? If so, such consent is generally disfavored; look for actual consent and question whether jurisdiction should be based on fictitious consent.

- If the defendant knew that certain actions, such as corporate registration, constituted consent to service on a particular state agent, that is more akin to actual consent.

- However, if the defendant can be said to have been unaware of the consent to appoint an agent for in-state service, such as is the case with non-resident motorist statutes, consent will be more suspect. In such a case, an ordinary minimum contacts analysis applies. Proceed to Part C.3.

b. **State Citizens**—Is the party challenging personal jurisdiction a citizen of the forum? If so, forum courts may exercise personal jurisdiction over that party as a state citizen. *Milliken v. Meyer*, 311 U.S. 457, 463 (1940).

c. **Non-resident Plaintiffs**—Is the party challenging personal jurisdiction the original plaintiff in the action? If so, that party has already consented to jurisdiction by choosing to bring the action in the forum. *Adam v. Saenger,* 303 U.S. 59, 67–68 (1938).

d. **Estoppel**—Is the defendant estopped from challenging jurisdiction for some reason? See *Ins. Corp. of Ireland v. Compagnie des Bauxites de Guinee*, 456 U.S. 694, 702 (1982) (finding the defendant to be estopped from challenging jurisdiction because of the defendant's refusal to cooperate with jurisdictional discovery orders); *Farmingdale Steer-Inn, Inc. v. Steer Inn Realty Corp.*, 274 N.Y.S.2d 379 (Sup. Ct. 1966) (defendant estopped from challenging jurisdiction after misrepresenting that it was registered to do business in the state).

3. *International Shoe* **Test**—if none of the above exceptions applies, then you must ask, Does the assertion of jurisdiction satisfy the standard of *International Shoe*?

    a. *In rem* **Actions**—is this an *in rem* action?

        i. If so, *Shaffer* has indicated that such actions will generally meet the minimum contacts standard (to use the language of *International Shoe*, these are isolated but directly related contacts that warrant jurisdiction).

        ii. If not, proceed to the next question.

    b. **Four-Position Matrix**—determine whether the contacts serving as the basis for jurisdiction are systematic and continuous or single and isolated and whether they are related or unrelated to the cause of action.

        i. **Continuous and Systematic and Related**—Personal jurisdiction is appropriate. *See Int'l Shoe*; **Keeton v. Hustler Magazine,** 465 U.S. 770 (1984).

        ii. **Continuous and Systematic but Unrelated**—Possible situation permitting general jurisdiction. Ask whether the contacts can be described as "substantial" and compare them with the contacts in the following two cases:

            • *Perkins v. Benguet*, 342 U.S. 437 (1952) provides the general jurisdiction standard and illustrates facts sufficient to support a finding of general jurisdiction.

            • *Helicopteros v. Hall*, 466 U.S. 408 (1984) provides facts insufficient to support general jurisdiction.

            • If the unrelated contacts are insufficient to support general jurisdiction, proceed to specific jurisdiction analysis to see if any related but isolated contacts also exist.

        iii. **Single & Isolated and Unrelated**—no personal jurisdiction.

iv. **Single & Isolated and Related**—this is a specific jurisdiction fact pattern. Proceed to the specific jurisdiction analysis.

4. **Specific Jurisdiction Analysis**—can specific jurisdiction be exercised over the defendant? The answer depends on a two-pronged analysis of minimum contacts and reasonableness:

   a. **Minimum Contacts**—are there minimum contacts between the defendant and the forum state?

      i. **Purposeful Availment**—has the defendant purposefully availed itself of the privilege of acting within the forum state such that it has received benefits and protections of the state? *Hanson v. Denckla*, 357 U.S. 235 (1958). If so, the minimum contacts requirement is satisfied. Proceed with the reasonableness analysis of Part C.4.b below.

         • This requirement assures that the defendant will be able to reasonably anticipate where its conduct will subject it to personal jurisdiction. *World-Wide Volkswagen Corp. v. Woodson*, 444 U.S. 286 (1980).

         • Purposeful availment cannot exist on the basis of the unilateral actions of parties other than the defendant. *World-Wide Volkswagen.*

      ii. **Intentional Torts**—if an intentional tort has been alleged, has the defendant intentionally targeted its tortious conduct at a forum resident and caused harm to that resident in the forum? If so, then personal jurisdiction over the defendant in the forum state is appropriate under the *Calder* "effects" test. *Calder v. Jones*, 465 U.S. 783 (1984).

      iii. **Contractual Contact**—does the defendant have a contractual relationship with a forum resident? If so, use contracts-plus analysis (i.e., consideration of the place of negotiation, execution, and performance of the contract) to consider whether the contract solicitation, negotiation, and course of conduct support finding of purposeful availment. **Burger King v. Rudzewicz**, 471 U.S. 462 (1985). *See also* **McGee v. Int'l Life Ins. Co.**, 355 U.S. 220 (1957). If purposeful availment is found, proceed with the reasonableness analysis of Part C.4.b below.

iv. **Stream-of-Commerce Cases**—if this is a stream-of-commerce case—meaning that a product of the defendant has caused harm to the plaintiff only after traveling through the stream of commerce—do the facts satisfy the O'Connor or Brennan standard for purposeful availment? **Asahi Metal v. Superior Court**, 480 U.S. 102 (1987).

- **O'Connor Standard**—the defendant must have intended for its product to be marketed in the forum state in order to have purposefully availed itself of the forum.

- **Brennan Standard**—the defendant merely must have been aware that its product would be marketed in forum state in order to satisfy the purposeful availment requirement of the *International Shoe* test.

- **Reasonableness Analysis**—if purposeful availment is found here, proceed with the reasonableness analysis of Part C.4.b below. If not, still proceed with the reasonableness analysis in light of the approach taken in *Asahi* where O'Connor analyzed reasonableness even after finding no purposeful availment.

v. **Quasi in Rem Cases**—is jurisdiction being asserted based on property located within the state? If so, you must still analyze the in-state property as you would any other contacts. Property ownership is considered an isolated contact for jurisdictional purposes. **Shaffer v. Heitner**, 433 U.S. 186 (1977).

vi. **Internet Cases**—is this a case where the contacts are through the Internet? If so, analyze whether the Internet contacts show purposeful availment.[50] If purposeful availment is found, proceed with the reasonableness analysis of Part C.4.b below.

- *Inset Systems v. Instruction Set, Inc.*, 937 F. Supp. 161 (D. Conn. 1996)—under *Inset*, the presence of a website advertising one's product is sufficient to establish purposeful availment in every state where the website is available. This approach has generally been repudiated by the courts.

- *Zippo Mfg. v. Zippo Dot Com*, 952 F. Supp. 1119 (W.D. Pa. 1997)—under *Zippo*, a website alone is not enough to support jurisdiction. The propriety of jurisdiction depends on the location of the site on the active/interactive/passive spectrum.[51]

  - **Passive**—is the website passive? If so, jurisdiction is not appropriate based on the website per *Zippo*.

  - **Active**—is the website active? If so, jurisdiction is appropriate under *Zippo*.

  - **Interactive**—is the website interactive? If so, then jurisdiction will *depend* on the degree of interactivity and the commercial nature of the website. A highly interactive

---

50. Internet-specific tests need not be used exclusively in one's analysis. If an intentional tort is alleged, the "effects" test of *Calder* can also be relevant. Even where an Internet-specific test is used, it should be done in the context of a traditional analysis and not in isolation. That means still considering purposeful availment and reasonableness rather than rote application of the *Zippo* sliding scale.

51. It should be noted that these classifications should really be used simply to determine whether the website satisfies the purposeful availment requirement. Thus, the better approach is to continue on with a reasonableness analysis after applying the *Zippo* test rather than reaching a conclusion solely based on the active/interactive/passive classification attached to the website.

commercial website will generally support personal jurisdiction.[52]

- **Express Aiming of Internet Activity**—most circuits evaluate Internet-mediated contacts by asking whether the Internet activity was specifically aimed at the forum state. If so, then the contact may be sufficient to establish purposeful availment if it gave rise to the cause of action. If not, see if there are forum contacts that can be evaluated under one of the other purposeful availment rubrics.

b. **Reasonableness**—if your analysis has indicated that the defendant has purposefully established minimum contacts with the forum state, then ask, "Would the exercise of jurisdiction be (un)reasonable?" Analyze with reference to the following five factors applied in *Asahi*, noting that a balancing of the first three of these factors is typically determinative. The balancing of these interests is somewhat a subjective exercise that depends on the facts.

   i. **Burden on the Defendant.** Would the inconvenience to the defendant be unconstitutionally burdensome, meaning it would impact the defendant's ability to mount a defense? A *yes* answer would weigh against reasonableness.

   ii. **State Interest.** Does the State have a strong interest in resolving the dispute? The state's interest is greater where its laws or policies are at stake, or where state citizens or corporations are involved. An affirmative answer here weighs in favor of reasonableness.

   iii. **Plaintiff Interest.** Does the plaintiff have a strong interest in obtaining relief in the forum? If so, that is a factor favoring reasonableness.

---

52. It may be worthwhile to ponder the difficulties with this approach when you are applying it on an exam. Shortcomings of the *Zippo* model include its focus on commercial websites, its outdated view of the nature of activity on the Internet, and the lack of clarity in the meaning of an "interactive" website and the jurisdictional consequences associated with operating such websites. *See* A. Benjamin Spencer, *Jurisdiction and the Internet: Returning to Traditional Principles to Analyze Network-Mediated Contacts*, 2006 U. ILL. L. REV. 71.

iv. **Systemic Efficiency.** Would jurisdiction promote the interstate judicial system's interest in efficient resolution of controversies?

v. **Furtherance of Social Policies.** Would jurisdiction promote the shared interest of the States in furthering fundamental substantive social policies?

ILLUSTRATIVE PROBLEMS

Here are a couple of problems that illustrate how this checklist can be used to resolve personal jurisdiction questions:

■ PROBLEM 1.1 ■

Xenon, Corp., a Delaware corporation with its principal place of business in California, is an oil distribution company that operates principally in North and South America. It entered a long-term Crude Oil Supply Agreement ("Agreement") with NG, Inc., an Oklahoma-based company incorporated in Oklahoma and Petroleos de Peru (PDP), the Peruvian state oil company based in Lima, Peru (PDP and NG generally did business together). The parties entered the Agreement at a meeting in NG's Houston office after months of negotiations, which also occurred in Texas at NG's Houston office (NG has several major oil production facilities in Texas that are supervised and managed out of the Houston field office). The Agreement was entered into in order to generate a market for PDP's and NG's crude oil through Xenon's extensive U.S. distribution and retail channels.

Under the terms of the Agreement, PDP and NG were supposed to supply crude to Xenon at an agreed discount rate compared with what the two charged on the open market. Over time however, Xenon came to believe that PDP and NG were overcharging it for crude and demanded repayment of the excess amounts paid. When PDP and NG refused payment, Xenon brought suit on the contract against NG and PDP in Texas federal court, demanding $100 million dollars in damages. Both defendants were served at their respective headquarters. Assume Texas has a long-arm statute permitting the exercise of jurisdiction over all parties to contracts negotiated and/or executed in Texas.

In response to the complaint, PDP and NG both filed motions to dismiss for lack of personal jurisdiction. How should the court rule?

Analysis

As an initial matter, it is worth noting that the first response of the defendants was to file motions to dismiss for lack of personal jurisdiction. Thus, neither defendant has waived its personal jurisdiction challenge. Because this is a case in federal court, Rule 4(k)(1)(A) seems to apply, which means that personal jurisdiction is determined with reference to whether a court of the state where the federal court sits—Texas—could exercise jurisdiction.[53] That question is answered by posing two separate questions. First, "Is jurisdiction appropriate under the Texas long-arm statute?" and second, "Is the assertion of jurisdiction constitutional?"

Regarding the long-arm statute, the Problem reveals that Texas courts may exercise jurisdiction over parties to contracts negotiated and/or executed in Texas. Here, the facts indicate that the contract was both negotiated and executed in Houston, Texas at NG's office. Thus, under the terms of the Texas long-arm statute, jurisdiction over both NG and PDP would be appropriate.

Because the terms of the long-arm statute are satisfied, we proceed to the constitutional analysis. Inquiring first into the existence of any traditional basis for jurisdiction, it appears that none apply. Both defendants are corporate entities and thus the in-state service rule does not apply. Further, the Problem does not indicate whether the Agreement contained a forum-selection clause of any kind, which would serve as consent to jurisdiction.

Thus, it is necessary to move on to the jurisdictional analysis set forth in *International Shoe*. To analyze the defendants' contacts

---

53. PDP is a foreign corporation and thus potentially could be covered by Rule 4(k)(2); however, this is not a federal question case so Rule 4(k)(2) does not apply.

with the forum state, Texas, we must first determine whether their contacts with Texas are systematic and continuous or sporadic and isolated. We must also determine whether their contacts are related or unrelated to the cause of action.

Taking NG's contacts first, its contacts with Texas appear to be fairly systematic and continuous. The Problem indicates that they have an office in Houston and that they have "several major oil production facilities" in Texas. Taken together, these types of contacts with the state could be described as systematic and continuous. However, if we were to attempt to exercise general jurisdiction on the basis of these contacts we would need to be able to characterize the contacts as "substantial" in the vein of those contacts found to be sufficient to exercise jurisdiction in *Perkins v. Benguet.* Here, the presence and operation of "several major oil production facilities" belonging to NG sounds pretty substantial and compares favorably with those contacts found to be sufficient in *Perkins.* Further, such contacts appear to be much more systematic and continuous than those in *Helicopteros.* However, courts have rarely found contacts to be sufficiently substantial unless they approach a level akin to domicile for individuals. Thus, one could conclude that general jurisdiction would not work here with respect to NG (although strong arguments could be made for a contrary result).

Is specific jurisdiction a possibility here with respect to NG? If we look at the Houston office as being a forum contact that is related to the contract claim plus the fact that the contract at issue was negotiated and signed there (we will set aside the oil production facilities as related contacts since we are not told that these facilities play a role in the performance under the contract), that would seem to be more of an isolated contact. As an isolated but related contact, the office could support personal jurisdiction if it satisfies the purposeful availment requirement and if jurisdiction would be reasonable. The office is certainly a purposeful forum contact of NG and it could reasonably anticipate having to answer in Texas for claims arising out of its dealings in that office. Regarding reasonableness, Texas arguably has some interest in the dispute given the signing of the contract there but the better argument seems to be that they have a slight interest given that none of the parties to the action are Texas citizens. The burden of Texas jurisdiction on NG would be slight, but Xenon has no particularly strong interest in litigating its claims there versus Oklahoma where NG can be found. Thus, on balance I would conclude that jurisdiction in Texas over NG would be unreasonable, but equally convincing arguments could be made in support of concluding that jurisdiction would be reasonable.

Moving on to the question of whether jurisdiction is appropriate over PDP, the Problem does not disclose any facts indicating a systematic and continuous connection with Texas. The only connection revealed is the negotiation and execution of the Crude Oil Supply Agreement in Texas. Thus, PDP's contacts can be described as isolated. However, the contacts are directly related to the cause of action, which is an action on the contract. With PDP's contacts being isolated but related, jurisdiction will be appropriate if the purposeful availment and reasonableness requirements can be satisfied.

Did PDP, through its forum-state contacts, purposefully avail itself of the privilege of conducting activities in Texas, thereby invoking the benefits and protections of its laws? Although the Court has upheld jurisdiction against parties who enter into contracts with forum residents, *see McGee; Burger King*, here PDP did not enter a contract with a forum resident but rather with a California and Delaware corporation with no disclosed connections with Texas. Although PDP did enter into negotiations in Texas and executed the Agreement there, none of the parties to the Agreement were Texas residents and performance under the Agreement did not bear any necessary relation to Texas, so far as the Problem discloses. None of the other means of establishing purposeful availment are present or relevant so it does not appear that PDP's contacts with Texas satisfy the purposeful availment requirement under the minimum contacts branch of *International Shoe*.

The lack of minimum contacts would typically end the inquiry, but Justice Brennan, under his sliding-scale approach, would proceed with an evaluation of the reasonableness factors to see whether they balance in favor of the plaintiff to such a degree that they can overcome the lesser showing made under the minimum contacts prong of the test. Here, Texas does not have any strong interest in this dispute because none of the parties are from Texas. Xenon has an interest in receiving relief but it can do so by pursuing its claims elsewhere, possibly in Oklahoma. The burden on PDP would be great given that it is based in Peru and would have to travel some distance to defend a case in Texas. Thus, it may be fairly concluded that jurisdiction over PDP in Texas would be unreasonable.

In sum, although general jurisdiction would probably not be available over NG based on its systematic and continuous contacts with Texas, specific personal jurisdiction probably would work based on its Houston office and the connection with the dispute. However, jurisdiction would not be appropriate over PDP due to its lack of minimum contacts with Texas and due to the fact that an exercise of jurisdiction over PDP in Texas would be unreasonable.

■ PROBLEM 1.2 ■

A Massachusetts company, ABC.com, sells a product called widget gears, gears that combine with a widget in order to make it work more effectively. ABC.com does not accept orders for its product through its website. However, ABC.com uses its website to advertise its product and a local Boston telephone number is listed on the website as a source for more information. ABC.com has received orders for its product through the mail and over the telephone from across the country. About 1.5% of its sales have been to Indiana customers.

Mort Davidson, an Indiana resident who holds a patent for a similar product sues ABC.com in Indiana federal court for patent infringement. Assume the federal patent statute contains no provision regarding service of process or personal jurisdiction. Further assume that Indiana's long-arm statute permits jurisdiction over those whose out-of-state or in-state conduct causes harm within the state. ABC.com moves to dismiss the action for lack of personal jurisdiction. Result?

Analysis

As this is a federal case, the first question is which provision of Rule 4 provides the standard for personal jurisdiction (ABC.com has not waived personal jurisdiction because it raised the jurisdictional challenge in its initial response). A federal statute is involved here, but the Problem discloses that it contains no special service or jurisdiction provision, rendering Rule 4(k)(1)(C) inapplicable. Thus, Rule 4(k)(1)(A) applies. Under that Rule, jurisdiction is appropriate here if Indiana courts could exercise jurisdiction.

Since the jurisdictional challenge was properly raised and not waived, the propriety of jurisdiction will have to be assessed with reference to the Indiana long-arm statute and the U.S. Constitution. Under the long-arm statute, it can be said that ABC.com's conduct, whether it can be described as having oc-curred outside or within Indiana, has caused harm within Indiana in the form of the alleged infringement of Davidson's patent. So the long-arm statute appears to be satisfied.

No traditional basis for jurisdiction applies here and thus a constitutional analysis is necessary. The constitutional analysis requires first determining whether the contacts are systematic and continuous or sporadic and isolated, and whether the contacts are related or unrelated to the cause of action. Here, the accessibility of ABC.com's website is a continuous presence within Indiana; how-ever, a website does not appear to be the type of contact that courts would deem to be systematic and continuous, since property ownership, though continuous, is viewed as an isolated contact under *Shaffer*. But here, ABC.com's connection to Indiana directly gave rise to the patent infringement claim. Thus, this Problem presents a potential specific jurisdiction case.

To determine whether specific jurisdiction is appropriate here, ABC.com must have demonstrated purposeful availment of

Indiana and the assertion of jurisdiction must be reasonable. Under the framework established by *Zippo*, purposeful availment can be found based on a website that is active or possibly if it is interactive. However, where a website is completely passive, the website will not support a finding of purposeful availment. Here, the facts reveal that the site is merely an advertisement, offering no means for site visitors to interact with it. Thus, the site can be classified as passive. As such, ABC.com cannot be said to have purposefully availed itself of Indiana through its website, at least under the *Zippo* framework.[54] Using the more sophisticated express aiming approach that many courts are using currently to analyze Internet contacts, one could argue that ABC.com's website was not specifically targeted at Indiana and thus conclude again that there is no purposeful availment based solely on the website.

However, the website is not the only forum-state contact of the defendant. The defendant also has sales of the infringing product to Indiana residents through the website and most importantly has been alleged to have committed patent infringement of a forum-state resident's patent. One can certainly reasonably anticipate being subject to jurisdiction for patent infringement in the jurisdiction where the allegedly infringing product is being sold and in the jurisdiction where the patent-holder resides (one might analogize the reasoning of *Calder* to the reasoning here, treating patent infringement like an intentional tort).

Looking to the reasonableness analysis, there is nothing patently unreasonable about requiring ABC.com to defend where its website has caused harm under the logic of *Calder v. Jones*. Plaintiffs should not have to travel to where their wrongdoers are located in order to redress harms done against them where they reside. Plus, given modern day technology and transportation

---

54. If the competing (but disfavored) *Inset* approach were applied instead, purposeful availment would result from ABC.com's delivery of its advertising website into Indiana (although *Inset* also involved the posting of a toll free telephone number, something that is absent here). Given ABC.com's interest in garnering sales from whatever source, including Indiana, and evidence that sales to Indiana customers have occurred, it seems reasonable to treat ABC.com as having purposefully availed itself of Indiana via its website, notwithstanding the results suggested by application of the *Zippo* test.

capabilities, the burden on ABC.com of defending itself in Indiana would probably not be constitutionally unreasonable.

Thus, I would feel comfortable concluding that jurisdiction over ABC.com is proper in Indiana based on its website, forum-state sales, and the status of the patent holder as a forum state resident. However, if primary attention is paid to the website, the majority approach to analyzing Internet contacts would likely hold that a passive website directed to all consumers nationwide rather than being aimed at Indiana would be insufficient to support jurisdiction in Indiana and would hold that ABC.com's motion to dismiss for lack of personal jurisdiction should be granted.

POINTS TO REMEMBER

- Do not forget to determine whether the state's long-arm statute permits jurisdiction if the case is in state court or in federal court where jurisdiction is being evaluated under state standards.

- Traditional bases and exceptions do not automatically confer jurisdiction, they simply provide instances where the exercise of jurisdiction would be constitutional. The relevant state long-arm statute must still be satisfied in order for jurisdiction to be exercised in those circumstances.

- When analyzing specific jurisdiction, try to do both the minimum contacts and the reasonableness analyses (an example is Justice O'Connor's *Asahi* opinion) to cover your bases. You can cite Justice Brennan's sliding-scale approach as the reason for such a belt-and-suspenders approach, but note that his approach is not the clear favorite of the Court. The Court has not quite come to terms with how to align the purposeful availment and reasonableness prongs of the *International Shoe* test.

- Fact patterns in exam questions won't necessarily fit into neat boxes. There may be Internet contacts and an intentional tort or a case may involve products placed in the stream of commerce and a contract with a forum resident. Be prepared to analyze cases across categories, synthesizing the analysis as necessary.

- Distinguish among different defendants. The jurisdictional fate of one does not necessarily apply to all.

- If there are alternate approaches to resolving or analyzing an issue (e.g., O'Connor v. Brennan in *Asahi*; Scalia v. Brennan in *Burnham*; *Inset v. Zippo*), acknowledge the existence of the alternate approaches, select one to apply, and explain your selection. Where one approach is preferred or enjoys majority support, that should be acknowledged and generally followed; however, if there are good reasons for following the alternative approach, do so and articulate why the alternative is better.

*

CHAPTER 2

Notice and the Opportunity to Be Heard

The Due Process Clause not only limits the permissible scope of a court's jurisdiction over parties to an action; it also provides for two of the most basic rights that a defendant has within our legal system: the right of the defendant to receive notice of and the opportunity to be heard in a lawsuit against it. This chapter will briefly sketch out the contours of these rights and provide a checklist for evaluating problems that can arise in this area.

REVIEW OF NOTICE

The Due Process Clause requires that one made a party to an action be notified of its pendency before a court is permitted to adjudicate that party's rights. The requirement of prior notice is similar to the requirement that a court have personal jurisdiction over a party in that the absence of either will prevent the court from being able to affect the party's rights. However, notice is a separate concept to which distinct standards apply. In *Mullane v. Central Hanover Bank & Trust Co.* the Supreme Court set forth the constitutional standard for adequate notice: notice reasonably calculated, under all the circumstances, to apprise interested parties of the pendency of the action and afford them an opportunity to present their objections.[1]

Under this standard, proper notice must convey sufficient information to notify the party of how and by when it should respond and must allow reasonable time to appear. Further, the means of giving notice must be such as one desirous of actually informing the party might reasonably adopt to achieve actual notice.[2] However, this does not mean that the method that is most likely to succeed is required nor does it mean that actual notice must be achieved.[3] Rather, the most reasonable means available is all that is necessary. If there is a better means that is available and reasonably practical, then it should be employed; but when a superior method is too expensive, time consuming, or burdensome, then it will not necessarily be required over more practical methods under *Mullane*. The method of service employed is what is important here; a constitutionally deficient procedure cannot be overcome by the fact that actual notice was received.[4]

For *in personam* actions, constructive notice by publication is generally not reliable because the chance of actual notice based on publication alone is slim. Thus, such notice is generally insufficient for *in personam* actions under *Mullane*.[5] However, in *Mullane* the Court indicated that for *in rem* or *quasi in rem* actions service by publication may be acceptable when accompanied by an attachment, but only if the names and addresses are unknown and not reasonably ascertainable.[6] Thus, it appears that service by publica-

---

1.   339 U.S. 306, 314 (1950).

2.   *Id.* at 315.

3.   Dusenbery v. United States, 534 U.S. 161, 162 (2002).

4.   *See, e.g.*, Wuchter v. Pizzutti, 276 U.S. 13, 24–25 (1928) (invalidating New Jersey's non-resident motorist statute on the ground that it failed to require the Secretary of State to communicate notice of the commencement of an action to nonresidents).

5.   *See* Tulsa Professional Collection Servs., Inc. v. Pope, 485 U.S. 478, 490 (1988) (hold-ing that service by publication is insufficient to notify prospective creditors to an estate when their identities are known or reasonably ascertainable).

6.   *See, e.g.*, Mennonite Bd. of Missions v. Adams, 462 U.S. 791, 798 (1983) ("When the mortgagee is identified in a mortgage that is publicly recorded, constructive notice by publication must be supplemented by notice mailed to the mortgagee's last known available address, or by personal service. But unless the mortgagee is not reasonably identifiable, constructive notice alone does not satisfy the mandate of *Mullane*.").

tion is acceptable only as a last resort only when no other alternative is available or reasonably practicable.

Application of *Mullane* is very fact-specific; a method of notification that may be appropriate under one set of facts can be inadequate under a different set of circumstances. For example, service by mail may provide constitutionally adequate notice ordinarily, but such service will be inadequate when the defendant is known to be incompetent[7] or if the mail returns with notice of non-delivery.[8] Similarly, posting notice on property might be adequate under some circumstances but it may be inadequate in an environment where it is known that the posting is likely to be removed.[9]

Rule 4 sets out methods of notice to be followed within the federal system. Compliance with the methods provided for in the rule is deemed to be compliant with the constitutional standard articulated in *Mullane*.

OPPORTUNITY TO BE HEARD REVIEW

The Due Process Clause also serves as the basis for the right of parties to be heard before a court makes any determination of their rights. In **Fuentes v. Shevin** the Supreme Court held that the opportunity to be heard must be given at a "meaningful time and in a meaningful manner."[10] The Court felt that in order for notice and the right to be heard to serve their purpose they must be granted at a time when the deprivation can still be prevented because a subsequent hearing cannot undo a wrongful deprivation. Thus, the Court in *Fuentes* held that the general rule was that an individual must be given an opportunity to be heard *before* he is deprived of any significant property interest.[11]

The Court subsequently backtracked on this view and migrated toward a three-part standard (borrowed from **Mathews v.**

---

7. Covey v. Town of Somers, 351 U.S. 141, 146 (1956).

8. Jones v. Flowers, 547 U.S. 220 (2006).

9. Greene v. Lindsey, 456 U.S. 444, 453–54 (1982).

10. 407 U.S. 67, 80 (1972).

11. *Id.* at 82–83.

Eldridge[12]) for determining the validity of pre-deprivation procedures in *Connecticut v. Doehr*.[13] First, courts are to consider the
nature of the property interest at stake, which requires courts to
evaluate the significance of the private interest that will be affected
by the prejudgment measure. Second, courts are to examine the
risk of erroneous deprivation through the procedures under attack
and the probable value of additional safeguards. These risks can be
mitigated by procedures that require the plaintiff to make some
showing of entitlement, that require that the plaintiff post a bond,
or that involve a judge in making the determination, but such
procedures need not be adversarial in nature.[14] Third, courts are to
consider the interest of the party seeking the prejudgment remedy
and if relevant, any ancillary interest of the government.

NOTICE AND THE OPPORTUNITY TO BE HEARD CHECKLIST

With that backdrop, here is the checklist for analyzing problems
involving the right to notice and the opportunity to be heard:

A.   NOTICE—was adequate notice given to the defendant? Was notice
reasonably calculated, under all the circumstances, to apprise
interested parties of the pendency of the action and afford them an
opportunity to present their objections? *See Mullane v. Central
Hanover Bank & Trust Co.*, 339 U.S. 306 (1950). To make this
determination, consider the following questions:

    1.   **Adequate Information**—does the notice convey sufficient in-
formation to notify the party of how and by when it should
respond?

       a.   **Yes.** If so, proceed to the next question.

       b.   **No.** If not, the notice is inadequate.

---

12.   424 U.S. 319, 335 (1976).

13.   501 U.S. 1 (1991).

14.   Mitchell v. W. T. Grant Co., 416 U.S. 600 (1974).

2. **Timeliness**—does the notice allow reasonable time to appear?

    a. **Yes.** If so, proceed to the next question.

    b. **No.** If not, the notice is inadequate.

3. **Method**—is the method of giving notice a method that one desirous of actually informing the party might reasonably adopt to achieve actual notice? To answer this question, ask, "Was the most reasonable means available employed?"

    a. **No.** If there is a better means that is available and reasonably practical, then it should be employed. This includes follow-up attempts to provide notice after discovering that notice has failed. *See **Jones v. Flowers***, 547 U.S. 220 (2006).

    b. **Yes.** Where a superior method exists but is too expensive, time consuming, or burdensome, then it need not be employed over more practical methods under *Mullane*. The notice given to the defendant was adequate.

B. **OPPORTUNITY TO BE HEARD**—does the pre-deprivation hearing comport with the constitutional requirements of due process? Apply the three-pronged test of *Connecticut v. Doehr*:

1. **Property Interest at Stake**—what is the nature of the private interest that will be affected by the deprivation? This question focuses on what kind of property is at stake—is it a house, a car, vacant land? So long as the property interest is not so minor as to be insignificant, it will be a protectable interest under the Due Process Clause. Further, property interests that are of vital importance to the defendant, such as housing or wages, will warrant greater pre-deprivation protections given their connection with the defendant's basic needs.

2. **Risk of Erroneous Deprivation**—what is the risk that the defendant will be wrongfully deprived of its property? The following are considerations that aid in, but are not completely determinative of, the resolution of this issue:

    a. **Showing**—what type of showing does the plaintiff have to make? The more that a plaintiff has to show to support his or her claim, the lower the risk of erroneous deprivation.

　　b.　**Bond**—is there a bond requirement? A bond requirement will tend to ensure that only plaintiffs with plausible claims will seek the property. The higher the bond requirement, the more likely the plaintiff's claim is to be non-frivolous, thus reducing the risk of erroneous deprivation.

　　c.　**Judge**—is the decision made by a judge or a non-judicial court official such as a clerk? Where a judge is involved in the decision, there is a better chance that the defendant will not be wrongfully deprived of its property.

3.　**Plaintiff's Interest**—what is the interest of the party seeking the prejudgment remedy and if relevant, any ancillary interest of the government? Does that party have a pre-existing interest in the property or a speculative interest? When the plaintiff's interest is less speculative there is less of a chance that the deprivation will be erroneous.

4.　**Your Analysis**—there are no across-the-board requirements here; you have to determine whether the protections that are in place provide the defendant with adequate protection given the nature of the defendant's property interest at stake and the strength of the plaintiff's alleged interest in the property.

ILLUSTRATIVE PROBLEMS

Now, here are some problems that will demonstrate how this checklist can be used to resolve notice and opportunity to be heard questions:

■ PROBLEM 2.1 ■

Stephen proceeds *in rem* against property purportedly owned by Ron, seeking to claim title over the property. Ron's name appears in the public records as the owner of record and his home address is provided therein. To notify Ron of the quiet title action, Stephen posts notice of the suit on the property to which he is claiming title, assuming that Ron will be apprised of the action if such notice is placed on land that he purports to own. The notice included the time and place of the initial hearing and was posted ten days before the hearing date.

Ron fails to appear in the action and Stephen obtains a default judgment against the property. Ron learns of the judgment and challenges it on the ground that the notice in the prior action was constitutionally deficient. Result?

Analysis

The question here is whether Stephen has provided constitutionally sufficient notice of the quiet title action to Ron, the record property owner. To be adequate, the notice must convey certain information in a timely fashion sufficient to permit Ron to respond and be heard. Further, the method of delivering service to Ron must be reasonably calculated under the circumstances to provide Ron with proper notice.

Here, the notice provided Ron with sufficient information regarding the time and location of the hearing to enable him to appear and defend himself. Similarly, the facts indicate that notice was posted 10 days prior to the hearing, which, if seen, would arguably have given Ron enough advance time to appear.

The problem here is with the method of notice. Although the Court has indicated that notice by posting or publication can be permitted for *in rem* actions under some circumstances, the Court has also held that such notice is inadequate where the names and addresses of property owners are known or ascertainable. Here, the facts show that the name and address of the property owner were ascertainable by reference to the county records. Because Stephen could have easily obtained information regarding the record owner's address, Stephen did not use the best means practicable or reasonably available. Thus, notice by posting was not reasonably calculated, under the circumstances, to provide notice to the owner of the land. As a result, Ron's challenge to the notice should succeed.

■ PROBLEM 2.2 ■

The city of Flanders has a local ordinance permitting the police to impound vehicles parked on the street that are determined to be "junk" vehicles that have been abandoned. A police officer who repeatedly sees a vehicle parked and unmoved over a one month period and who determines based on the appearance of the vehicle that it is junk or has been abandoned, may mark the vehicle with a warning sticker indicating that it will be removed in two weeks time unless the owner moves the car or informs the police that it is not junk. After two weeks pass, a police tow truck may remove it.

The city invoked this procedure with respect to Leonard's 1955 Plymouth. Leonard had parked the car lawfully on the street in front of his house but was traveling abroad for a three-month extended vacation. On his return he learned that his car had been impounded and destroyed. He sued to recover damages, arguing that the city's deprivation procedure was constitutionally infirm for failing to provide him with a reasonable opportunity to be heard. How should the court rule on Leonard's constitutional challenge?

Analysis

The issue here is whether the city's deprivation procedure is defective for failing to provide an adequate hearing. Under *Connecticut v. Doehr* a three-pronged test is used to determine the adequacy of pre-deprivation procedures. First, the nature of the property interest at stake is evaluated. Here, the property interest is Leonard's car. Presumably, this car is his primary means of transportation and is likely important in enabling Leonard to travel to work or to shop for necessities, although the facts do not disclose this information. In any event, it can be assumed that one's interest in their vehicle is a sufficiently important interest such that it should not be violated absent adequate measures designed to protect the owner against a wrongful deprivation.

Next, under *Doehr*, we are to consider the extent to which the procedure protects Leonard against a wrongful deprivation. Here, the procedure allows one month to go by before a car is marked as possible junk. Further, a warning sticker is posted on the vehicle itself, giving the owner two weeks notice that the vehicle will be removed and an opportunity to contact police to prevent the removal. Arguably, these mechanisms provide the owner with sufficient time to learn of the threat to his property and the opportunity to prevent removal by the city by contacting the police. However, the police are not required to make any type of showing establishing that the vehicle is abandoned junk. The determination is made by the police themselves without having to make any showing to a judicial official or clerk. Although the police use guidelines to make their own determination of the vehicle's status, no information has to be presented to impartial third parties. Additionally, there is no bond or any other security requirement that the police have to put in place to protect the owner should the scrapping of the car be done in error. Finally, there is no opportunity for the owner to be heard after the deprivation occurs, which would at least give the owner a chance to reclaim the vehicle before it is destroyed. Thus it appears that the protections against erroneous deprivation are inadequate.

The final check under *Doehr* is the interest of the party seeking the deprivation in the property in question. Here, the city apparently has an interest in keeping public streets clear of abandoned junk vehicles. However, the city asserts no proprietary interest in the vehicles themselves. The governmental interest of keeping the streets free of junk vehicles is a valid and important interest but cannot be permitted to allow the city to remove all cars parked on the street and destroy them without employing constitutionally sufficient safeguards to protect mistaken deprivations.

Given these deficiencies in the city's junk vehicle removal procedures, Leonard's constitutional objection should be upheld.

POINTS TO REMEMBER

- A party must receive notice of the pendency of an action before its rights can be determined.

- It is not just the method of notice that matters, but the content and timing of the notice as well.

- Actual notice is not required; only a method reasonably calculated to apprise the party of the action is required. This requires the best means *practicable*, not the best means available.

- Service by publication is generally not adequate for *in personam* actions. For *in rem* or *quasi in rem* actions constructive notice or notice by publication is permissible only if the names and contact information of the property owners are not known or reasonably ascertainable.

- The Due Process Clause does not require pre-deprivation hearings nor does it require that deprivation decisions be reviewed by a judge. Rather, the standard is a fact-dependent one that principally considers the protections against erroneous deprivation and the interests at stake. Thus, procedures that are adequate in one context may be inadequate in another.

CHAPTER 3

Subject Matter Jurisdiction

In addition to the requirement of personal jurisdiction discussed in Chapter 1, and the requirement of proper notice reviewed in Chapter 2, a federal court must be authorized to hear the type of dispute being brought before it. Such authority is referred to as subject matter jurisdiction. The authority of federal courts to hear certain types of cases derives from Article III of the U.S. Constitution. Congress has extended much of the authority granted in Article III to lower federal courts through various statutory enactments located principally in Title 28 of the U.S. Code.

SUBJECT MATTER JURISDICTION REVIEW

The main categories of federal subject matter jurisdiction studied by first-year law students are diversity jurisdiction, federal question jurisdiction, supplemental jurisdiction, and removal jurisdiction.

Diversity Jurisdiction

Diversity jurisdiction is governed by 28 U.S.C. § 1332, which provides that in disputes where the amount in controversy *exceeds*

$75,000,[1] federal courts have jurisdiction to hear cases involving suits between citizens of different States, suits between citizens of a State and citizens of foreign states (aliens), citizens of different States where aliens are also parties, and foreign states as plaintiffs and citizens of a State.

A key task in determining whether diversity jurisdiction exists is identifying the citizenship of the parties to the action. Citizenship for individuals is determined based on their *domicile*; to establish domicile a person must be physically present in a place and have the intention of remaining there indefinitely. For a corporation, citizenship is based on its state of incorporation and the state where its principal place of business is located,[2] meaning that a corporation potentially can have citizenship in two states for diversity jurisdiction purposes. Some courts use the so-called *nerve center* test (the location of decision-making authority) to determine the location of the corporation's principal place of business for jurisdictional purposes while others use the *muscle* test (the location of the bulk of the corporation's production or service activities). A third group of courts use the *total activity* test, in which a court "considers a variety of factors, such as the location of the corporation's nerve center, administrative offices, production facilities, employees, etc., and it balances these factors in light of the facts of each case."[3] Partnerships and unincorporated associations, however, are citizens of every state and country of which its partners or members are citizens.[4] Finally, legal representatives are deemed to be citizens only of the state of the party whom they represent.[5]

Courts have interpreted § 1332 as requiring *complete diversity*, meaning that no party on one side of a case may share state citizenship with any party on the other side of the case.[6] However,

---

1. Keep in mind that the statute requires an amount in controversy in excess of $75,000. That means claims totaling $75,000 will not qualify.

2. 28 U.S.C. § 1332(c)(1).

3. *Amoco Rocmount Co. v. Anschutz Corp.,* 7 F.3d 909, 915 (10th Cir. 1993).

4. *See* Lincoln Property Co. v. Roche, 546 U.S. 81, 84 n.1 (2005) (citing Carden v. Arkoma Associates, 494 U.S. 185, 189, 192–97 (1990)).

5. 28 U.S.C. § 1332(c)(2).

6. Strawbridge v. Curtiss, 7 U.S. 267 (1806). Complete diversity can be destroyed where a

if there is evidence that a party has been improperly or collusively named simply for the purpose of creating a basis for diversity jurisdiction, the citizenship of the collusively or improperly named party may be ignored for diversity purposes.[7]

In figuring the amount in controversy for purposes of § 1332, compensatory and punitive damages can be counted. Prejudgment interest and costs, however, are not to be included in this figure. To satisfy the amount in controversy requirement, a single plaintiff is free to aggregate any of her claims against a single defendant or jointly liable defendants. However, a single plaintiff may not aggregate claims against multiple defendants where joint liability is not alleged, and multiple plaintiffs may not aggregate their claims to reach the jurisdictional amount unless their claim is based on a common undivided interest (for example, they are seeking damage to property they own jointly as tenants by the entirety).

Provided there is complete diversity and the amount in controversy is satisfied, a court will have jurisdiction to hear the claim.

Federal Question Jurisdiction

Federal question jurisdiction is governed generally by 28 U.S.C. § 1331, which provides for federal jurisdiction over all cases arising under federal law.[8] This provision has been interpreted to require that a claim contain an essential federal element that appears on the face of the plaintiff's well-pleaded complaint.[9] That means that federal defenses or claims raised by the defendant will be insufficient to serve as the basis for federal question jurisdiction. A claim will contain an essential federal element when the cause of action is created by federal law, or when the plaintiff's right to relief on a

---

permanent resident alien is an adverse party to a citizen of the state where the alien resides. 28 U.S.C. § 1332(b). Note also that in class actions, citizenship for purposes of diversity jurisdiction is determined with reference only to the named plaintiffs, not all members of the class. *See* Devlin v. Scardelletti, 536 U.S. 1, 10 (2002).

7. 28 U.S.C. § 1359.

8. Special federal question statutes exist as well. *See, e.g.,* 28 U.S.C. § 1334 (bankruptcy actions); 28 U.S.C. § 1337 (antitrust actions); 28 U.S.C. § 1338 (patent and copyright actions).

9. Louisville & Nashville R.R. Co. v. Mottley, 211 U.S. 149 (1908).

state-based cause of action depends on the application or interpretation of federal law, provided a substantial federal interest is at stake.[10] Unfortunately, there appears to be no uniform standard for determining whether a federal interest is sufficiently substantial. In practice you would refer to the law of the circuit to see how this requirement has been interpreted and applied. What seems to be clear, at least, is that the existence of a federal constitutional question is generally viewed as creating a substantial federal interest.[11] The Supreme Court has also suggested that a controversy respecting the construction and effect of federal laws will be considered substantial.[12]

Supplemental Jurisdiction

Supplemental jurisdiction is provided for in 28 U.S.C. § 1367, which outlines the circumstances under which claims that independently cannot qualify for federal jurisdiction can nonetheless be heard in federal court. Specifically, a state claim lacking an independent basis for federal jurisdiction may be heard in federal court on the basis of supplemental jurisdiction when it is part of the same case or controversy as a claim in the case that does have its own basis for federal jurisdiction (the "freestanding" claim), which the Supreme Court has defined as meaning that the claims arise from a *common nucleus of operative fact*.[13] The only proviso is that in an action where the court's sole basis of jurisdiction is diversity of citizenship, there can be no supplemental jurisdiction over state-based claims made by plaintiffs against those made parties under Rules 14, 19, 20, or 24.[14] Neither can there be supplemental jurisdiction over non-federal claims by parties joined under Rule 19 or Rule 24 where jurisdiction would be contrary to the standards

---

10. Merrell Dow Pharms. Inc. v. Thompson, 478 U.S. 804 (1986); Smith v. Kansas City Title & Trust Co., 255 U.S. 180, 199 (1921). The Supreme Court more recently stated, where a state-law claim is concerned, "[T]he question is, does a state-law claim necessarily raise a stated federal issue, actually disputed and substantial, which a federal forum may entertain without disturbing any congressionally approved balance of federal and state responsibilities." Grable & Sons Metal Prods. Inc. v. Darue Engineering & Mfg., 545 U.S. 308, 314 (2005).

11. *Kansas City Title*, 255 U.S. at 202.

12. *Grable & Sons*, 545 U.S. at 315.

13. 28 U.S.C. § 1367(a); United Mine Workers of America v. Gibbs, 383 U.S. 715 (1966).

14. 28 U.S.C. § 1367(b).

of Section 1332, the diversity statute.[15]

Section 1367(c) sets forth several circumstances under which supplemental jurisdiction should not be exercised as a prudential matter, even though the requirements of the statute are satisfied. These include when the supplemental claim presents a novel or complex issue of state law, the state claim predominates over the federal claims, the federal claim has been dismissed, or when other circumstances are present, such as the likelihood of jury confusion resulting from hearing the claims jointly.[16]

Removal Jurisdiction

Removal jurisdiction is governed by 28 U.S.C. § 1441. Under the removal statute, a defendant in a state court action may have the case transferred (the proper term is "removed") to the federal district court for the district geographically embracing the location of the state court if the case could have been brought in federal court originally.[17] That means that the standards governing federal subject matter jurisdiction are relevant to an analysis of whether removal is permissible. The requirement that the case could have originally been brought in federal court to be removable also means that removal can only be based on the plaintiff's claims; removal is not possible on the basis of the defendant's counter-claims or defenses. Where the claims qualify for diversity, federal question, or supplemental jurisdiction, they may be removed to federal court, with several restrictions.

First, defendants from the same state as the court hearing the case may not remove actions to federal court unless jurisdiction would be founded on a claim that arises under federal law.[18] Second, all defendants must agree to removal, or no removal is possible.[19] Third, removal is only possible if defendants comply

---

15. *Id.* The Supreme Court has held, however, that the language of § 1367(b) permits supplemental jurisdiction over claims by plaintiffs joined either under Rule 23 (the class action rule) or Rule 20 (the permissive party joinder rule). *See* Exxon Mobil Corp. v. Allapattah Servs., Inc., 545 U.S. 546 (2005).

16. 28 U.S.C. § 1367(c).

17. 28 U.S.C. § 1441(a).

18. 28 U.S.C. § 1441(b).

19. Chicago, Rock Island & Pac. Ry. Co. v. Martin, 178 U.S. 245 (1900).

with the time limits prescribed in the removal statute.[20]

Procedurally, a defendant can remove a case simply by filing a notice of removal with the relevant federal court and in the state court where the case is pending.[21] Parties who believe the removal to be erroneous can then move in the federal court to remand the issue to state court, provided such a motion is made within thirty days of the filing of the notice of removal.[22]

 ## SUBJECT MATTER JURISDICTION CHECKLIST

The following checklist, which consists of a series of steps suggested by the statutes and case law, will help you determine whether a claim can be heard in federal court:

A. **ORIGINAL FEDERAL COURT JURISDICTION**—is there original jurisdiction over the claim by the plaintiff?

    1. Diversity Jurisdiction—does the action satisfy the requirements of 28 U.S.C. § 1332 such that the court may hear the case on the basis of diversity?

        a. **Citizenship of the Parties**—what is the citizenship of each of the parties in the action?

            i. **Individuals**—citizenship for individuals is determined based on their domicile; to establish domicile a person must be physically present in a place and have the intention to remain there indefinitely.

            ii. **Corporations**—for a corporation, citizenship is based on its place of incorporation and the place where its principal place of business is located. 28 U.S.C. § 1332(c)(1).

---

20. 28 U.S.C. § 1447(c).   **22.** 28 U.S.C. § 1447(c).
21. 28 U.S.C. § 1446(a).

iii. **Partnerships and Unincorporated Associations—** partnerships and unincorporated associations are citizens of every state and country of which its partners or members are citizens.

      iv. **Legal Representatives—**legal representatives are deemed to be citizens only of the state of the party whom they represent. 28 U.S.C. § 1332(c)(2).

b. **Diverse Parties—**are the parties diverse in one of the enumerated ways identified in § 1332?

      i. Are the adverse parties citizens of different states (the District of Columbia, Puerto Rico, and U.S. Territories are treated as states under § 1332)? If so, the parties are diverse; proceed to Part A.1.c.

      ii. Does the case involve a state citizen versus an alien? If so, the parties are diverse; proceed to Part A.1.c.

      iii. Does the case involve citizens of different states with aliens as additional parties on either side or both sides (remember that permanent resident aliens are treated as state citizens for purposes of destroying diversity)? If so, the parties are diverse; proceed to Part A.1.c.

      iv. Does the case involve a foreign state as a plaintiff versus a state citizen? If so, the parties are diverse; proceed to Part A.1.c.

      v. **Not permissible**: alien v. alien; state citizen + alien v. alien; alien v. alien + state citizen; state citizen v. permanent resident alien from same state.

c. **Complete Diversity—**are all of the parties on one side of the action diverse from all of the parties on the other side of the action? (Aliens can be from the same country.) *Strawbridge v. Curtiss*, 7 U.S. 267 (1806).

      i. **Yes**. If so, then complete diversity as is required exists.

      ii. **No**. If not, there is not complete diversity and there can be no diversity jurisdiction over the claim.

d. **Collusive Joinder—**is there evidence that a party has been improperly or collusively named simply for the purpose of creating a basis for diversity jurisdiction? If so, the citizenship of the collusively or improperly named party may be ignored for diversity purposes. 28 U.S.C. § 1359.

e. **Amount in Controversy**—is the claim for more than $75,000? 28 U.S.C. § 1332(a). If so, and the diversity of citizenship requirement has been satisfied, then diversity jurisdiction exists. Consult the following questions in determining the amount in controversy:

   i. **Punitive Damages Included**—are there punitive damages that can be added in to reach the jurisdictional amount?

   ii. **Costs and Prejudgment Interest Excluded**—are there costs and prejudgment interest that need to be excluded before evaluating whether the amount in controversy is satisfied? Contract interest may be included.

   iii. **Aggregation**—can the plaintiff's separate claims be aggregated to satisfy the amount in controversy? Only if one of the following circumstances exists:

   - There are multiple claims by one plaintiff against one defendant.

   - There are multiple plaintiffs asserting an undivided interest.

   - Claims alleging joint and several liability against multiple defendants are valued based on the entire amount claimed.

2. **Federal Question Jurisdiction**—does the action satisfy 28 U.S.C. § 1331 or one of the other statutes conferring federal question jurisdiction?

   a. **Essential Federal Element**—does the claim contain an essential federal element such that it arises under federal law?

      i. **Creation Test**—is the claim created by or brought pursuant to federal law?

      - **Yes.** If so, the claim arises under federal law; proceed to Part A.2.b.

      - **No.** If not, proceed to the next question.

ii. **Substantial Federal Interest Test**—if the claim is a state law claim, does the plaintiff's right to relief depend upon application or interpretation of federal law? If so, is the federal interest implicated "substantial"?

- **Yes.** If so, the claim contains an essential federal element provided the exercise of federal jurisdiction would not disturb any congressionally approved balance of federal and state responsibilities. *See Grable & Sons Metal Prods. Inc. v. Darue Eng'g & Mfg.*, 545 U.S. 308, 314 (2005). Proceed to the next question.

- **No.** If not, then the claim lacks an essential federal element and federal question jurisdiction does not exist.

b. **Well-Pleaded Complaint Rule**—does the essential federal element appear on the face of the plaintiff's well-pleaded complaint? *Louisville & Nashville R.R. v. Mottley*, 211 U.S. 149 (1908). If so, federal question jurisdiction is appropriate.

i. **Federal Responses Ignored**—are there anticipated or actual federal defenses or counterclaims presented that must be ignored for purposes of assessing the propriety of federal question jurisdiction?

ii. **Artful Pleading Doctrine**—is the presence (or absence) of a federal element genuine or artfully pleaded?

B. SUPPLEMENTAL JURISDICTION—if a claim does not qualify for diversity or federal question jurisdiction, does the claim qualify for supplemental jurisdiction under 28 U.S.C. § 1367?

1. **Section 1367(a)**—does the broad grant of supplemental jurisdiction in § 1367(a) apply to the claim?

a. **Freestanding Claim**—is there a claim over which the court has original jurisdiction? (See analysis *supra* Part A).

b. **Common Nucleus of Operative Fact**—is the supplemental claim at issue based on the same common nucleus of operative fact as the freestanding claim? *United Mine Workers of America v. Gibbs*, 383 U.S. 715 (1966).

2. **Section 1367(b)**—if § 1367(a) is satisfied, does § 1367(b) nonetheless bar supplemental jurisdiction in this case?

   a. **Diversity Claim?** Is the court's jurisdiction based solely on diversity?

      i. **No.** If not, § 1367(b) will not prevent supplemental jurisdiction.

      ii. **Yes.** If so, proceed to next question.

   b. **Supplemental Claim by Plaintiff?** Does the supplemental claim at issue consist of a claim by the plaintiff or by plaintiffs joining the case under Rule 19 or 24?

      i. **No.** If the claim is not made by the plaintiff or by a Rule 19 or Rule 24 plaintiff, then § 1367(b) will not prevent supplemental jurisdiction. Note that claims by plaintiffs joined under Rule 23 or Rule 20 may enjoy supplemental jurisdiction, provided the complete diversity rule is not violated.

      ii. **Claim by a Rule 19 or 24 Plaintiff.** If the claim is by a plaintiff joined under Rule 19 or Rule 24, the claim will not qualify for supplemental jurisdiction if such jurisdiction would be inconsistent with the requirements of the diversity jurisdiction statute.

      iii. **Claim by a Plaintiff.** If the claim is by the original plaintiff, then proceed to the next question.

   c. **Against Certain Joined Parties?** Is the claim against persons made parties under Rule 14, 19, 20, or 24?

      i. **No.** If not, § 1367(b) will not prevent supplemental jurisdiction.

      ii. **Yes.** If so, supplemental jurisdiction is not permissible.

3. **Discretionary Basis for Denial of Jurisdiction?** If § 1367(b) is not an obstacle, are one of the circumstances of § 1367(c) present such that supplemental jurisdiction should not be exercised?

   a. **Novel State Issue.** Does the supplemental claim involve a novel or complex state issue?

b. **State Claim Predominates.** Does the state claim substantially predominate over the federal claim (e.g., the bulk of the evidentiary showing will relate to state issues; the federal claim is minor compared with state claims)?

c. **Federal Claims Dismissed.** Have the federal claims been dismissed?

d. **Other Circumstances.** Are there other exceptional circumstances that would suggest that the supplemental claims should not be heard in federal court (e.g., jury confusion)?

C. **REMOVAL JURISDICTION**—if the case has already been filed in state court, may the defendant remove the case to federal court?

  1. **Original Jurisdiction**—would the federal district courts have original jurisdiction over the *plaintiff's* claims if they were filed in federal court? 28 U.S.C. § 1446(a).

  a. **Yes.** If so, the case may be removable, provided other requirements are met. Proceed to the next question if the case is a diversity action; proceed to Part C.5 if jurisdiction would be based on the presence of a federal question.

  b. **No.** If not, the case is not removable.

  2. **Time Limit**—have thirty days passed since the defendant received service of the initial pleading setting forth the removable claim or notice of a change in the removability of the case? 28 U.S.C. § 1446(b).

  a. **Yes.** If so, then the defendant has waived the right to remove the case.

  b. **No.** If not, proceed to the next question.

  3. **Diversity Basis**—if the claim could have been brought in federal court based only on diversity, is the defendant who is seeking removal a citizen of the state where the case has been brought? 28 U.S.C. § 1441(b).

  a. **Yes.** If so, removal is improper.

  b. **No.** If not, removal may be proper. Proceed to the next question.

4. **Defendant Unanimity**—have all of the defendants agreed to removal? *Chicago, Rock Island & Pac. Ry. Co. v. Martin*, 178 U.S. 245 (1900).

    a. **No.** If not, the court will remand after removal.

    b. **Yes.** If so, removal will be proper.

5. **Federal Question Basis**—if the claim could have been brought in federal court based on federal question jurisdiction, then the claim is removable, provided there is defendant unanimity and the 30-day time limit for removal has not expired.

6. **Motion to Remand**—if an action has been removed can a party seek to remand the case to state court? This can be done only if a motion to remand is filed within 30 days of the filing of the notice of removal.

ILLUSTRATIVE PROBLEMS

Let's now work through the following problems to see how this checklist can be used to resolve questions involving subject matter jurisdiction:

■ PROBLEM 3.1 ■

ABC Corp., a Delaware corporation with its principal place of business in Maryland wants to sue two members of its board of directors, Mike and Jennifer, for fraud. Mike is a citizen of Virginia and Jennifer is a citizen of New York. ABC claims $75,000 in damages against Mike and $75,000 in damages against Jennifer, because each of them separately defrauded the company out of $75,000. Can ABC bring its case in federal court?

Analysis

Because no claim based on federal law is involved here (and there appears to be no essential federal element), jurisdiction will depend on whether the requirements for diversity jurisdiction can be satisfied. The first requirement is that the adverse parties be completely diverse. That requires that each plaintiff must be diverse from each defendant. Here, the plaintiff, ABC, is considered a citizen of Delaware and Maryland under § 1332. The two defendants are both citizens of different states than ABC, Virginia and New York. Thus, the complete diversity requirement is satisfied.

The next hurdle is that the amount-in-controversy requirement must be satisfied. In order for there to be diversity jurisdiction, the amount in controversy must *exceed* $75,000 exclusive of interest and costs. Here, ABC's claim is for $75,000 against Mike and $75,000 against Jennifer. Because neither of these claims independently satisfy the amount in controversy requirement, jurisdiction will only be proper if the two claims can be aggregated to reach the jurisdictional amount. Claims against multiple defendants can only be aggregated for diversity purposes if joint liability is being asserted against them. Here, the facts indicate that the two board members separately defrauded the company out of $75,000 each. There is no allegation that the two jointly bilked the company for $150,000 and that one or both of them are together liable for that entire amount.

Because joint liability is not asserted here and the separate claims do not exceed the required amount in controversy, diversity jurisdiction is unavailable and the case cannot be brought in federal court.

■ PROBLEM 3.2 ■

Victor, a Delaware citizen, sues Xavier, also a Delaware citizen, in Delaware state court for breach of a patent licensing contract for failing to pay a $5,000 licensing fee that was due on the contract last month. In response, Xavier claims that Victor's patent is invalid. Twenty days after Victor's complaint was filed, Xavier also filed a notice of removal and the case was removed to Delaware federal court.

One week after removal, Victor moved to remand the case back to Delaware state court. How should the court rule on Victor's motion?

Analysis

This problem requires both a removal analysis and a federal question analysis. In order for a case to be removable to federal court, the case must have been one that could have been brought in federal court originally based on the plaintiff's claim. Here, the plaintiff alleged the breach of a patent licensing contract, to which Xavier raised the invalidity of the patent as a defense. Could such a claim have been brought originally in federal court?

Given that the parties are not diverse and the amount in controversy does not exceed $75,000, the claim could be heard in federal court only if the requirements of federal question jurisdiction could be satisfied. In order for there to be federal question jurisdiction over a claim, the claim must have an essential federal element that appears on the face of the plaintiff's complaint. An essential federal element can exist if the claim is created by federal law or if Victor's right to relief depends upon application or interpretation of federal law. This claim is not created by federal law but rather is based on state contract law. However, it is possible that federal law must be applied to determine the validity of the claim. Validity of the patent has been put in issue by Xavier as a defense. This does not seem to matter, though, because the critical issue in this case is the validity of the licensing contract, not of the patent. If Victor owns the patent, then whether as a matter of federal law it is valid or not is irrelevant. If Xavier contracted to pay Victor for something he owns then he has to pay Victor as a matter of contract law. Thus, it appears that no essential federal element exists here.

Further, there is no federal element that appears within Victor's complaint. The fact that Xavier raises a federal defense does not matter for jurisdictional purposes. Because federal question jurisdiction must be based on the plaintiff's complaint and not responses of the defendant, and no essential federal element appears in Victor's complaint, there can be no federal question jurisdiction over Victor's claim against Xavier.

Because the case could not have been brought initially in federal court, it may not properly be removed. Victor's motion for remand was made within the requisite time limit and thus the court should grant Victor's motion to remand the case to state court.

■ PROBLEM 3.3 ■

Oz, a citizen of Ohio, sues Ann, his employer and also a citizen of Ohio, in federal court alleging that Ann violated federal civil rights statutes by permitting her subordinates to engage in sexual harassment of Oz. Oz joins (under Rule 20) Liz as a defendant, a co-worker and citizen of Ohio, who actually engaged in the harassment. Because Liz is not Oz's employer, state tort law is the basis of Oz's claim against Liz. Oz seeks $75,001 in damages against Liz. Does the federal court have subject matter jurisdiction over Oz's claims against Ann and Liz?

Analysis

Two claims are involved here: one against Ann, the employer, and another against Liz, the co-worker. Regarding the claim against Ann, this claim is based on federal law because it is alleging a violation of federal civil rights law. As such, Oz's claim against Ann qualifies for federal question jurisdiction.

Regarding Oz's claim against Liz, no federal question presents itself because the facts reveal that Oz's claim against her is based on state tort law. Because Oz and Liz are not diverse, the court will only have jurisdiction over the claim if the requirements of the supplemental jurisdiction statute can be satisfied. The first requirement for supplemental jurisdiction is that the supplemental claim be part of the same case or controversy as is involved in the freestanding claim over which the court does have original jurisdiction. To make that determination, we ask whether the claims arise out of a common nucleus of operative fact. Here, the claims do share a common nucleus of operative fact because they both arise out of the instance of sexual harassment perpetrated against Oz.

Under § 1367 the claim against Liz is thus entitled to supplemental jurisdiction unless one of the exceptions outlined in § 1367(b) applies. Here, because jurisdiction over the freestanding claim is based on federal question jurisdiction, the exceptions of § 1367(b) do not apply; thus, supplemental jurisdiction over Oz's claim against Liz is appropriate.

POINTS TO REMEMBER

- For diversity jurisdiction there must be *complete diversity,* meaning no plaintiff may be from the same state as any defendant; thus, be sure to check the citizenship of all parties on all sides.

- Remember that the amount in controversy must *exceed* $75,000; thus, claims for $75,000 will be insufficient.

- When aggregating claims to achieve the jurisdictional amount in controversy involving either multiple plaintiffs or defendants, only do so when the multiple parties are suing jointly on an undivided interest or are being sued jointly.

- The defendant's claims or defenses cannot form the basis for federal question jurisdiction nor can they be the basis for removal jurisdiction. Both types of jurisdiction must be based on the plaintiff's complaint.

- Where diversity serves as the sole basis of jurisdiction, remember to analyze both § 1367(a) & (b) to determine if supplemental jurisdiction is proper. When the supplemental claims are by plaintiffs against certain joined parties (parties joined under Rules 14, 19, 20, or 24) they will not qualify for supplemental jurisdiction nor will claims by plaintiffs joined under Rules 19 or 24, if jurisdiction over such claims would be inconsistent with the requirements of diversity jurisdiction.

CHAPTER 4

Venue

here is a fourth requirement—in addition to personal jurisdiction, proper notice, and subject matter jurisdiction—that
must be satisfied before a court may hear a case: venue.
Venue rules are rules of convenience; rules of venue function as a
means of allocating judicial business among different courts within
the same system (among cities/counties within states; among districts within the federal system).

REVIEW OF VENUE DOCTRINE

Whether venue is proper in the federal system depends on
compliance with statutory venue requirements.[1] The general venue
statute is found at 28 U.S.C. § 1391, but numerous other special
venue statutes exist.[2] If a special venue statute applies, Section 1391
is either inapplicable or supplementary, depending upon the
language of the special statute. Further, removal actions do not
have to satisfy the terms of the general venue statute[3] nor do claims
qualifying for supplemental jurisdiction; venue in the case of
supplemental claims is determined with reference to the accompa-

---

1. All of the standards for venue are evaluated at the time the action is commenced.

2. *See, e.g.*, 28 U.S.C. § 1391(d) (venue for
suits against aliens); 28 U.S.C. § 1400 (patent

and copyright suits); 28 U.S.C. § 1401
(shareholder derivative suits); 28 U.S.C.
§ 1402 (suits against the United States).

3. 28 U.S.C. § 1441(a).

nying freestanding claims. Finally, venue can be waived, either by prior agreement or by failing to challenge improper venue initially.[4]

Under the general venue state, venue is proper in any district indicated by either of two tests as outlined in Section 1391(a)(1) & (2) (diversity only actions) or Section 1391(b)(1) & (2) (non-diversity only actions). The first test (§ 1391(a)(1) & (b)(1)) provides that venue is proper in the district where any defendant resides (individual residence is equivalent to domicile for most courts), provided the defendants all reside within the same state. For corporate defendants,[5] they are deemed to reside in district where they are subject to personal jurisdiction, or, where multi-district states are involved, to reside in the district "with which its contacts would be sufficient to subject it to personal jurisdiction if that district were a separate State."[6] The second test (§ 1391(a)(2) & (b)(2)) makes venue proper in any district where a substantial part of the events or omissions giving rise to the cause of action occurred. If property is at issue, then venue is proper in the district where a substantial part of the property is located.

If neither of these tests can be satisfied, meaning that neither rule gives you a proper venue, then venue is appropriate as determined by either of two "fallback" provisions. For diversity-only actions, if a proper venue does not exist based on the first two tests, then venue is proper wherever any defendant can be subject to personal jurisdiction.[7] For non-diversity cases, venue is proper simply in any district where any defendant "may be found,"[8] a standard that has not been truly distinguished from the "subject to personal jurisdiction" standard of the diversity fallback provision.

Many students become confused regarding the circumstances under which the fallback provision can be used to determine

---

4. *See* FED. R. CIV. P. 12(h)(1). The mechanics of making pre-answer motions are covered in Chapter 9 below.

5. Unincorporated associations are treated like corporations under the venue statute. Denver & G.W.R. Co. v. Bhd. of R.R. Train-men, 387 U.S. 556 (1967). Treatment of partnerships and legal representatives for venue purposes has not been clarified.

6. 28 U.S.C. § 1391(c).

7. 28 U.S.C. § 1391(a)(3).

8. 28 U.S.C. § 1391(b)(3).

venue. The confusion typically arises because the fact pattern will present a case in a particular federal district court and then ask whether venue is proper there; students will proceed to see if the identified district can qualify as a proper venue under either of the first two tests. Where neither of the first two tests lays venue in the district identified in the question, students mistakenly look to the fallback provision to see if it will lay venue in the desired district where the case was filed. This approach is wrong. You can only refer to the fallback provision if neither of the first two tests gives you *any* venue. If they do suggest a venue, then that is the end of the matter, regardless of whether the tests give you the venue that you want. When either test lays venue in districts besides the one where the case has been filed, venue is improper in that district and the case should be dismissed or transferred.

Transfer of Venue

An action may be transferred to an alternate venue within the federal system under 28 U.S.C. § 1404. Either party may seek a transfer and such can be granted by the court "for the convenience of the parties and witnesses" and "in the interest of justice."[9] However, transfers can only be made to districts where the case could have been originally brought, regardless of whether the defendant now consents to suit in the alternate forum.[10]

If venue is initially improper, a defendant can move for dismissal of the action under Rule 12(b)(3); however, the court has the authority under 28 U.S.C. § 1406 either to dismiss the case or transfer it to a district with proper venue, again if the court deems such a transfer to be in the interest of justice.

In diversity actions, the applicable state law in the transferring court follows the transfer and is to be applied in the court receiving the transferred case, provided the transfer occurs under Section 1404(a).[11] Where federal law applies, however, most courts hold

---

9. 28 U.S.C. § 1404(a). The court can also order a transfer on its own motion.

10. Hoffman v. Blaski, 363 U.S. 335 (1960).

11. Van Dusen v. Barrack, 376 U.S. 612 (1964). After transfers under 28 U.S.C. § 1406(a) the transferee court applies the

that the receiving court need not adhere to interpretations of federal law that would have been binding on the transferring court but rather must apply federal law as it exists within the receiving jurisdiction.[12]

Forum Non Conveniens

Forum non conveniens is a common law (court-created) doctrine that permits the dismissal of a case over which a court has jurisdiction and venue on the ground that practical factors indicate that it should be heard in another court and that court is outside of the same judicial system. This doctrine differs from transfer of venue in that a transfer is appropriate when practical factors suggest another more convenient forum and that forum is within the *same* judicial system.

In order to obtain a dismissal on forum non conveniens grounds, two requirements must be satisfied. First, there must be an adequate alternative forum available for the case.[13] The applicability of less favorable law will not undermine the status of an alternate forum as adequate for purposes of the forum non conveniens doctrine.[14] Second, there must be a showing that interests of convenience to the parties and certain public interests argue in favor of the alternative forum notwithstanding plaintiff's choice of the current forum.[15] These public and private interests include the location of the events giving rise to the dispute, the location of witnesses and evidence, the applicable law, and the ability to compel others to participate in the action as witnesses or parties.[16]

---

law applicable in that court rather than the law of the transferor court.

12. Variances in federal law between two federal districts would arise if the district courts were within different federal circuits and those two circuits interpreted a particular matter of federal law differently.

13. Gulf Oil Corp. v. Gilbert, 330 U.S. 501 (1947).

14. Piper Aircraft Co. v. Reyno, 454 U.S. 235 (1981).

15. *Gilbert,* 330 U.S. 508–09.

16. *Id.*

VENUE CHECKLIST

With these principles in mind, here is the venue checklist:

A. **WAIVER**—has the party challenging venue waived the challenge? If so, then venue is proper.

    1. **Forum Selection Clause**—is there a forum selection clause that covers the situation and binds the parties involved? Such a clause would typically prevent a party from challenging venue that is proper under the clause.

    2. **Failure to Object**—has the party challenging venue already made a response to the complaint without challenging venue such that the challenge is waived under Rule 12(h)?

B. **SPECIAL VENUE STATUTE**—is there a special venue statute that applies? If so, then venue must be evaluated under the special statute, not § 1391.

    1. **Title 28**—is there a provision within Title 28 that carves out special venue provisions for certain types of cases?

        a. **United States as Defendant**—is this a suit against the United States? If so then venue is governed by § 1402.

        b. **Federal Interpleader**—is this a federal interpleader action? If so then venue is governed by § 1397.

        c. **Copyright and Patent Actions**—is this a copyright or patent action? If so then venue is governed by § 1400.

        d. **Shareholder Derivative Suit**—is this a shareholder derivative suit? If so then venue is governed by § 1401.

        e. **Alien Defendant**—is one of the defendants an alien person or a foreign corporation? If so then venue is governed by § 1391(d) (the alien venue provision).

    2. **Other Federal Statute**—is this a case arising under a particular federal statute? If so, the provisions of that statute should be consulted to determine whether it includes a special venue provision.

C. **GENERAL VENUE STATUTE**—if no waiver has occurred and no special venue provision applies, then apply the general venue statute (28 U.S.C. § 1391).

1. **First test under the general venue statute:** Do all the defendants reside within the same state?

   a. Identify the residency of each defendant.

      i. *Individuals*—residency is equated with citizenship (domicile) in most courts.

      ii. *Corporations*—resident in districts where they are subject to personal jurisdiction. For multi-district states, resident only in those districts where they would be subject to personal jurisdiction were the district a separate state.

   b. If all defendants reside in the same state, venue is proper in a district where any of the defendants reside.

   c. Continue on to the next test because it could possibly present another viable alternative venue.

2. **Second test under the general venue statute:** Is there a district where a substantial part of the events or omissions giving rise to the claim took place or where property that is the subject of the action is located?

   a. **Yes.** If so, venue is proper in any such districts.

   b. **No.** If not, and venue could not be determined based on the first test, proceed to determine whether venue is possible under the fallback provision.

3. **Fallback Provision**—if no proper venue can be identified based on the first two tests, then determine venue with reference to the fallback provisions of 28 U.S.C. § 1391.[17]

   a. **Diversity Cases**—if this is a diversity-only case, is there a district where any defendant is subject to personal jurisdiction? If so, venue is proper in any of those districts.

   b. **Non-Diversity Cases**—if this is not a diversity-only case, ask whether there is a district where any defendant can be found. If so, venue is proper in any of those districts.

D. **Transfer of Venue**—if venue is improper, can the case be transferred to another district? 28 U.S.C. §§ 1404, 1406.

---

17. 28 U.S.C. § 1391(a)(3) & (b)(3).

1. **Jurisdiction and Venue in Transferee Court?** Is the transfer being made to a district, within the same judicial system, where the action could have been brought initially?

   a. **No.** If not, then the case may not be transferred to that district.

   b. **Yes.** If so, proceed to the next question.

2. **Convenience and Justice?** Would a transfer be "[f]or the convenience of the parties and witnesses" (§ 1404 only) and "in the interest of justice" (§ 1404 & § 1406)? If so, then the court may transfer the case to the other district.

E. **Forum Non Conveniens**—Have the two prerequisites for a dismissal on forum non conveniens grounds been met?

   1. **Adequate Alternate Forum**—is there a forum outside of the federal system that is available for the prosecution of plaintiff's claim? If no adequate alternate forum exists, a dismissal for forum non conveniens is not proper. *Gulf Oil Corp. v. Gilbert*, 330 U.S. 501 (1947).

      a. **Unfavorable Law**—will the plaintiff face less favorable law in the alternate forum? If so, that is no impediment to recognition of the forum as a viable alternative. *Piper Aircraft Co. v. Reyno*, 454 U.S. 235 (1981).

      b. **Bar to Relief**—are the doors to the courts virtually closed to the plaintiff for some reason, preventing the ability to seek relief in the alternate venue? If so, then the alternate venue might not qualify as an adequate available alternative.

   2. **Public and Private Interests**—do private and public interests weigh in favor of having the case heard in the alternate forum? *Gulf Oil Corp. v. Gilbert*, 330 U.S. 501 (1947).

      a. **Private Interest Factors**—the following factors should be used to evaluate the viability and desirability of hearing a case in a proposed alternate forum:

         i. Location of the events giving rise to the case;

         ii. Availability of compulsory process for attendance of the unwilling;

   iii. Ability to implead other parties in the court;

   iv. Ability to take a view of premises involved in the dispute;

   v. Ease and cost of access to sources of proof, which depends on the location of relevant witnesses and documentary evidence; and

   vi. Enforceability of a judgment if one is obtained.

  b. **Public Interest Factors**—the following factors reflect interests of the government and local community of the proposed alternate forum that should be considered in determining whether hearing the case in that forum would be desirable:

   i. Whether the dispute involves local people or events; and

   ii. Whether the dispute is likely to be decided under the local law of the forum.

ILLUSTRATIVE PROBLEM

Here is a problem that will illustrate how this checklist can be used to resolve venue questions:

■ PROBLEM 4.1 ■

Xenon, Corp., a Delaware corporation with its principal place of business in California, is an oil exploration, production, and distribution company that operates principally in North and South America. In July 1990, Xenon entered a long-term Crude Oil Supply Agreement ("Agreement") with Astra Group, a joint venture between NG, Inc., an Oklahoma-based company incorporated in Oklahoma, and Texacorp, an oil company based in Houston, Texas. The parties entered the Agreement at a meeting in NG's Houston office after months of negotiations, which also occurred in Texas at NG's Houston office (NG has several major oil production facilities in Texas that are supervised and managed out of the Houston field office). Houston is located within the Southern

District of Texas. The Agreement was entered into in order to generate a market for Texacorp's crude oil through Xenon's extensive U.S. distribution and retail channels.

Under the terms of the Agreement, Texacorp was supposed to supply crude to Xenon at an agreed discount rate compared with what it charged on the open market. Over time however, Xenon came to believe that Texacorp was overcharging it for crude and demanded repayment of the excess amounts paid. When Texacorp and NG refused payment, Xenon brought suit on November 1, 2004, on the contract against NG and Texacorp in the Western District of Texas, demanding $100 million in damages. Both defendants were served at their respective headquarters. Assume Texas has a long-arm statute permitting the exercise of jurisdiction over all parties to contracts negotiated and/or executed in Texas.

In response to the complaint, Texacorp and NG both filed motions to dismiss for improper venue. How should the court rule?

Analysis

The first step in analyzing this problem is to determine whether Texacorp or NG have waived the right to object to venue. The facts do not disclose the existence of a forum selection clause so the parties cannot be said to have consented laying venue in the Western District of Texas. Because the defendants have challenged venue as their initial response to the complaint, it appears that their right to object to venue has not been waived under Rule 12(h).

Having preserved the right to object, the next step is to see whether a special venue statute applies. Because this is an ordinary contract dispute based on diversity jurisdiction and there are no alien defendants, no special venue statute applies and we can proceed with an analysis under § 1391(a). The first possible venue is the state where the defendants reside, provided all defendants reside in the same state. Residency of corporations is determined by § 1391(c), which provides that a corporation resides in the district where they would be subject to personal jurisdiction were that district a separate state. Here, NG has an office in the Southern District; given that this action arises out of contract negotiations occurring in the Houston office, NG probably would be subject to personal jurisdiction in the Southern District. Thus, for purposes of venue, NG can be considered to be a resident of the Southern District of Texas and thus a resident of Texas. Texacorp is based in Houston and so it would also be considered a resident of the Southern District of Texas. Because the defendants do all reside within the same state, venue would be proper in any district where any of the defendants reside. Here that would be the Southern District of Texas, not the Western District. Thus § 1391(a)(1) does not indicate that the Western District of Texas would be a proper venue.

Section 1391(a) next permits venue to lie in any district where a substantial part of the events giving rise to the claim occurred. Here, the contract was negotiated in the Southern District of Texas and performances of the obligations of the contract appear to be located in Houston and California, the location of the seller (Texacorp) and buyer (Xenon) under the agreement. So, it appears that venue is proper in the Southern District of Texas and possibly the district where Xenon's principal place of business is in California (the Southern District of California).

Because a proper venue can be determined based on § 1391(a)(2), no recourse to the "fallback" provision of § 1391(a)(3) may be had. Thus, the available proper venues for this action are the Southern District of Texas and the Southern District of California, but not the Western District of Texas. The defendants' objection to venue should thus be upheld.

POINTS TO REMEMBER

- Always check to see if any venue objections have been waived by consent or under Rule 12(h).
- Defendants must all reside in the same state for venue to be proper based on their districts of residence.
- Sections 1391(a)(3) and (b)(3) are *fallback* provisions, meaning these provisions may only provide the basis for venue where the other provisions fail to identify *any* proper venue.

- Transfers of venue are only proper to judicial districts *within the same judicial system* where the case could have originally been brought.

- Forum non conveniens dismissals are only proper when the more appropriate forum is outside of the judicial system where the case was filed. The court systems of each state, the federal courts, and foreign courts are all part of separate judicial systems.

*

CHAPTER 5

The *Erie* Doctrine—Ascertaining the Applicable Law in Federal Courts

Once a case has gotten into federal court, one of the issues the court will face is what law to apply to the various issues that will require resolution in the case. Identifying the applicable law in federal question cases is simple: federal law generally applies to the resolution of all legal issues, whether they are labeled substantive, procedural or otherwise. The more challenging inquiry is the determination of what law applies in diversity cases.

ERIE DOCTRINE REVIEW

Congress, through the Rules of Decision Act, has provided, "[T]he laws of the several states, except where the Constitution or treaties of the United States or Acts of Congress otherwise require or provide, shall be regarded as the rules of decision, in cases where they apply."[1] In the early case of *Swift v. Tyson*,[2] the Supreme Court interpreted this language to require federal courts to apply the statutory law of states but not state court decisional law expounding upon common law principles.[3] However, that view of the meaning

---

1. 28 U.S.C. § 1652.
2. 41 U.S. 1 (1842).
3. 41 U.S. 1, 18 (1842) ("In the ordinary

use of language it will hardly be contended that the decisions of Courts constitute laws.").

of "[t]he laws of the several states" was rejected many years later by the Court in **Erie Railroad Co. v. Tompkins.**[4] The approach adopted in *Swift* had resulted in mischievous instances of forum shopping and disparate bodies of law between federal courts and the state courts where they were located. To address these issues, the *Erie* Court overruled *Swift* and held that the Rules of Decision Act required application of the written and unwritten substantive law of the states in diversity cases.

The *Erie* decision was based in part on a suggestion that federal courts lacked the constitutional authority to develop substantive rules of common law applicable in a state because Congress lacked such authority. The Court indicated that the ability to develop substantive common law rules was a privilege not delegated to Congress in Article I of the U.S. Constitution and thus was the exclusive province of the states, presumably under the Tenth Amendment. This limitation on federal authority to develop substantive common law applicable in diversity cases was not seen, however, as limiting the authority of the federal government to develop and enforce procedural law applicable in the federal courts.[5]

Unfortunately, the distinction between substantive and procedural law in many cases was not as easily discernible as it had been in *Erie* itself, which involved common law tort principles concerning duties to trespassers. In subsequent cases, the Court wrestled with how to formulate principles that would guide it and lower courts in determining whether a particular state's rule of law had to be followed in federal diversity cases.

In **Guaranty Trust Co. v. York**[6] the Court had to determine whether an expired state statute of limitations period prevented a federal court sitting in equity from hearing the diversity case. Discarding the substance versus procedure framework, the Court

---

4. 304 U.S. 64 (1938).

5. *See id.* at 92 (Reed, J., concurring) ("[N]o one doubts federal power over procedure.").

6. 326 U.S. 99 (1945).

announced a new test: whether disregarding the state law that would be controlling in an action on the same claim in a state court would significantly affect the result of the litigation in federal court. This approach came to be known as the "outcome determinative" test and was rooted in the idea that federal courts hearing cases solely because of the diversity of citizenship of the parties in effect serve as state courts, and the outcome in the federal court should not differ substantially from what the outcome would be were the case tried in a state court.

The outcome determinative test had its shortcomings. Primarily, there was no limit to which rules of law, whether procedural or substantive, could be considered as having an impact on the outcome of litigation. Every rule of law could feasibly be so described. In **Byrd v. Blue Ridge Rural Electric Cooperative, Inc.**[7] the Court addressed this issue by revising the standard. *Byrd* involved the question of whether a judge (the state rule) or jury (the federal rule) would decide certain factual issues in the case. Applying what can be termed a balancing approach, the Court indicated that outcome determinativeness must be evaluated with reference to the importance of the state rule to state substantive policies and the countervailing federal interests embodied in the federal practice. Finding no evidence that the state practice of judicial decision-making was central to the state's worker compensation regime, the Court had no difficulty favoring the federal practice of letting a jury make the determination, in light of the announced federal policy—embodied in the Seventh Amendment—of assigning disputed issues of fact to juries.

The Court again addressed the question of whether to apply state or federal law in **Hanna v. Plumer**,[8] a case involving the applicability of former Rule 4(d)(1) of the Federal Rules in the face of a contrary state practice. Application of the state rule—which required personal in-hand service on executors of estates—would result in a dismissal of the action while using the federal rule would permit it to go forward. Thus, the decision not to apply the state

---

7.   356 U.S. 525 (1958).   8.   380 U.S. 460 (1965).

rule was clearly outcome determinative. However, the Court indicated that the *Erie* line of cases was not applicable to the situation where there is a valid and applicable Federal Rule of Civil Procedure involved. Under such circumstances, said the Court, if the Federal Rule is valid under the Rules Enabling Act[9] and the U.S. Constitution, and the rule is directly applicable to the issue at hand, then the federal court is bound to apply it.

In order to be valid under the Constitution, the rule must regulate matters that are procedural or capable of being classified as either substantive or procedural. In turn, to determine whether a federal rule truly regulates procedure, courts ask whether the rule regulates "the judicial process for enforcing rights and duties recognized by substantive law and for justly administering remedy and redress for disregard or infraction of them."[10] To be valid under the Rules Enabling Act, the rule must again be procedural in that it pertains to the enforcement of legal rights rather than their establishment, and the rule may not "abridge, enlarge or modify" any substantive right.[11] The *Hanna* Court, finding Rule 4(d)(1) to be directly applicable and consistent with the Constitution and the Rules Enabling Act, held that the federal rule and not the contrary state rule had to be followed.[12]

The Court in *Hanna* also expounded on the *Erie* doctrine, articulating how application of *Erie* to the facts of *Hanna* would lead to the same result, were it applicable. Rather than simply asking whether application of federal law would result in a different outcome than would result from application of the state law, the key question is whether application of federal law would undermine the "twin aims" of *Erie*: "discouragement of forum-shopping and avoidance of inequitable administration of the laws."[13] The Court

---

9. 28 U.S.C. § 2072.

10. Sibbach v. Wilson & Co., 312 U.S. 1 (1941).

11. 28 U.S.C. § 2072.

12. The Court addressed the applicability of a federal statute (rather than a Federal Rule) in the face of conflicting state law in *Stewart Organization, Inc. v. Ricoh Corp.*, 487 U.S. 22 (1988), holding that the federal statute, where it is procedural, governs under the Supremacy Clause of the Constitution (Article VI).

13. *Hanna*, 380 U.S. at 468.

then said that the forum-shopping concern is to be addressed from the perspective of prospective litigants, meaning that the court asks whether application of the federal practice would affect the choice of a state versus a federal forum at the outset of the litigation, not at the point where the court's decision is being made. In *Hanna,* the Court concluded that the difference between the state and federal rules at issue in that case would not be of much relevance to the selection of a forum *ex ante* and that permitting application of the federal rule would not result in inequitable administration of the laws between state and federal courts. Thus, an analysis under *Erie* as restated by the *Hanna* Court would support the application of the federal rule.

Hanna called into question an earlier decision of the Court, **Ragan v. Merchants Transfer & Warehouse Co.,**[14] which held that Federal Rule 3 (which indicates that an action commences at the time the complaint is filed) was inapplicable to the tolling of a state statute of limitations in a diversity action where there was a contrary state rule tolling the statute upon receipt of service. The viability of *Ragan* was uncertain because *Hanna* indicated that *Erie* doctrine was inapplicable when there was a valid and controlling Federal Rule involved and that in such a case the Federal Rule must be followed. In **Walker v. Armco Steel Corp.**[15] the Court affirmed the validity of *Ragan* by indicating that Rule 3 was not directly applicable to the tolling of statutes of limitations in diversity actions but rather was designed to govern the date from which various timing requirements of the Federal Rules begin to run. Because Rule 3 was not controlling of the issue before the court, there was no conflict between state and federal law and the *Hanna* analysis did not apply. Finding that the failure to apply the state rule would result in inequitable administration of the law, the Court held that the state rule should be applied.

The *Erie* line of cases thus present two strains of analysis for questions of whether to apply state versus federal law. One strain— the *Hanna* analysis—applies to situations where a contrary Federal

---

14. 337 U.S. 530 (1949).   **15.** 446 U.S. 740 (1980).

Rule of Civil Procedure or federal statute applies and proceeds with an analysis under the Rules Enabling Act and/or the U.S. Constitution. The other strain—a traditional *Erie* analysis—applies where the conflicting federal practice is not embodied in a rule or statute and resolves the conflict with reference to the Court's analysis under the Rules of Decision Act. Such an analysis initially determines whether the issue can be readily classified as substantive or procedural, with the state practice prevailing if the issue is substantive. If there is no clear answer, however, then the analysis proceeds to determining whether either of the "twin aims" of *Erie* is undermined; that is, would application of the federal practice lead to forum-shopping or the inequitable administration of the laws in federal versus state courts. Finally, the competing practices should be evaluated under the *Byrd* balancing approach to determine the respective policy interests underlying the state and federal practices; strong interests on either side may impact the choice of which law to apply. Understanding this distinction between a *Hanna* analysis and a classic *Erie* analysis and the circumstances under which each analysis applies is critical to mastering the *Erie* doctrine.

ERIE DOCTRINE CHECKLIST

With that backdrop, here is the checklist for analyzing problems presenting questions implicating the *Erie* doctrine:

A. **DIVERSITY ACTION**—is this a federal question case or a diversity case? There is no need to conduct an *Erie* or *Hanna* analysis for federal question cases.[16] If this is a diversity case, then proceed to the next question.

B. **PRESENCE OF A FEDERAL RULE OR STATUTE**—*Hanna* instructs that the initial question should be whether the issue before the court is

---

16. If there are both diversity and federal question claims within a single action, the *Erie* doctrine applies to the determination of what law to apply to the diversity claims.

potentially covered by a Federal Rule of Civil Procedure or federal statute as opposed to an uncodified federal practice.

1. **Federal Practice Not Embodied in a Statute or Rule**—if no federal rule or statute is at stake, the federal practice will have to be evaluated with reference to the *Erie* analysis below in Part E.

2. **Federal Practice Embodied in a Statute or Rule**—if there is either a federal statute or rule in the picture, proceed to the next question.

C. CONTROLLING FEDERAL RULE OR STATUTE—is the federal rule or statute sufficiently broad to control the issue before the court? ***Walker v. Armco Steel Corp.***, 446 U.S. 740 (1980). That is, is the federal rule or statute "intended or designed to govern the issue at hand" such that "the rule's purposes would be served by applying it"?[17]

1. **Not Controlling**—in the absence of a controlling federal rule or statute, the determination of whether to apply state law must be made with reference to the *Erie* analysis below in Part E.

2. **Controlling**—if the federal rule or statute was designed to control the issue before the court, proceed with the *Hanna* analysis.

D. *HANNA* ANALYSIS

1. **Direct Conflict**—is the applicable federal rule or statute in "direct collision" with the law of the relevant state? ***Hanna v. Plumer***, 380 U.S. 460 (1965).

   a. **No Direct Conflict**—if there is no direct conflict between an applicable federal rule or statute and state law then the federal law should be applied and no further analysis is required.

   b. **Direct Conflict**—if there is a direct conflict between an applicable federal rule or statute and an otherwise applicable state law, then proceed to the next question.

---

17. Westen & Lehman, *Is There Life for* Erie *After the Death of Diversity?*, 78 MICH. L. REV. 311, 342 (1980).

2. **Constitutionality of the Federal Rule or Statute**—does the rule regulate matters that are procedural or capable of being classified as either substantive or procedural? To determine whether a federal rule really regulates procedure ask whether the rule regulates "the judicial process for enforcing rights and duties recognized by substantive law and for justly administering remedy and redress for disregard or infraction of them." *Sibbach v. Wilson & Co.*, 312 U.S. 1 (1941).

   a. **The Federal Rule/Statute Regulates Substance**—if the federal rule or statute at issue regulates clearly substantive matters, then it may not be enforced in lieu of conflicting state law in diversity cases.

   b. **The Federal Rule/Statute Regulates Procedure**—if the rule or statute regulates procedural matters, or if it can be classified as both procedural and substantive, then the constitutional standard is satisfied.

      i. **Federal Statute?** If a federal statute is at issue, and it has been deemed to be procedural, there is no need to determine compliance with the Rules Enabling Act. The analysis is complete and the federal statute should be applied. *Stewart Org. Inc. v. Ricoh Corp.*, 487 U.S. 22 (1988).

      ii. **Federal Rule?** If a Federal Rule is at issue, proceed to the next question.

3. **Compliance with the Rules Enabling Act**—if a Federal Rule is at issue, does the rule comply with the Rules Enabling Act?

   a. **Rules Defining Legal Rights**—does the Federal Rule define legal rights or simply define the judicial process by which such rights are enforced?

      i. **Defines Legal Rights**—if the Federal Rule defines legal rights, then it is substantive and may not be applied in lieu of an applicable state law.

      ii. **Defines Enforcement of Rights**—if the Federal Rule merely pertains to the means of enforcing legal rights, then it is procedural. Proceed to the next question.

   b. **Abridgement of State Substantive Rights**—does the Federal Rule "abridge, enlarge or modify" any substantive right?

i.   **No.** If not, the rule complies with the Rules Enabling Act and is valid. The federal rule should be applied.

      ii.   **Yes.** If so, proceed to the next question.

   c.   **Procedural Interests Advanced?** If it appears that substantive rights are modified, can it be said that the Federal Rule advances clear procedural interests and only "incidentally affects litigants' substantive rights?" ***Burlington N. Ry. v. Woods***, 480 U.S. 1 (1987).

      i.   **Yes.** If so, then the rule complies with the Rules Enabling Act and is valid. The federal rule should be applied.

      ii.   **No.** If not, the rule violates the Rules Enabling Act and should yield to conflicting state law.

E. ***ERIE* ANALYSIS**—if no valid federal statute or Rule covers the issue before the court, then the question becomes, "Should the federal practice in question or the conflicting state practice be applied?"

   1.   **Substance v. Procedure Test**—can the issue be readily labeled as substantive and thus beyond the scope of federal courts to regulate within states?

      a.   **Substantive Rules of Common Law**—do the conflicting rules prescribe substantive duties and obligations, such as those embodied in the law of torts, contracts and property, as opposed to the mere "form and mode" of enforcing those duties and obligations?

         i.   **Yes.** If so, the federal legal rule may not be applied and must yield to conflicting state law, regardless of whether the state law is embodied in statutes or the decisions of state courts.

         ii.   **No.** If not, then the next set of questions must be considered to determine which rule should be applied.

   2.   **Modified Outcome–Determinative Test**—if the competing state and federal legal rules are not readily susceptible to classification as either substantive or procedural, then the outcome-determinative test as modified by *Hanna* should be applied.

a. **Forum Shopping Encouraged?** Would application of the federal standard impact a plaintiff's decision regarding whether to file suit in federal or state court?

    i. **Yes.** If so, the *Erie* policy of discouraging forum shopping is disserved. Proceed with the *Byrd* balancing approach to determine if there are any countervailing federal policies that warrant application of the federal legal rule notwithstanding its promotion of forum shopping.

    ii. **No.** If not, proceed to the next question.

b. **Inequitable Administration of the Laws Likely?** Would application of the federal legal rule result in "substantial" variations between outcomes in state and federal courts?

    i. **Yes.** If so, the *Erie* policy of avoiding inequitable administration of the laws is disserved. Proceed with the *Byrd* balancing approach to determine if there are any countervailing federal policies that warrant application of the federal standard notwithstanding its promotion of inequitable administration of the laws.

    ii. **No.** If not, then neither of the "twin aims" of *Erie* are implicated and the federal practice should be followed.

3. *Byrd* **Balancing Approach**—outcome determinativeness must be evaluated against the substantive policy interests furthered by the respective state and federal practices. To do so, ask the following questions:

a. **State Substantive Policy Furthered?** Is the state practice "bound up with the definition of the rights and obligations of the parties," such that the practice furthers some substantive state policy?

    i. **Yes.** If so, then it must be determined whether there is a countervailing federal policy that would warrant application of the federal practice. Proceed to the federal interest analysis below.

    ii. **No.** If not, then the presence of a federal policy that will be furthered by application of the federal rule will allow the court to ignore the state practice. Proceed to the next question to take a look at the federal policy interest at stake.

b. **Countervailing Federal Interest?** Does the federal legal rule promote an important federal substantive policy interest that outweighs the significance of the policy underlying the state legal rule?

   i. **Yes.** If there are important substantive policy interests that are furthered by the federal legal rule that are more important than the state interests at stake, the federal legal rule should be followed.

   ii. **No.** If there are only slight federal substantive policy interests at stake as compared with the substantive policies furthered by the state practice, the state legal rule should be followed.

ILLUSTRATIVE PROBLEMS

Now, here are some problems that will enable us to see how this checklist can be used to resolve *Erie* doctrine questions:

■ PROBLEM 5.1 ■

New Jersey has a statute that prohibits the entry of default judgments in actions on a debt. New Jersey passed the statute to curb the use of the courts to collect on debts owed to persons involved in organized crime. Several years ago, suspected participants in organized crime operations began suing to recover debts owed to them, using fear of reprisals to prevent defendants from appearing in court and thereby obtaining default judgments.

In Federal Court, Rule 55 provides that a default shall be entered when a defendant has failed to plead or otherwise defend as provided by the rules.

Michael, a New Yorker, sues James, a New Jersey citizen and owner of a local pizzeria, to recover on a debt of $80,000 in federal court. Fearing for his life, James does not appear to defend himself.

Michael moves for entry of default and a default judgment. How should the court rule on Michael's motion?

Analysis

The first question to ask is whether this is a federal question or a diversity case. From the facts, we can quickly see that the basis for this suit being in federal court is diversity of citizenship, being that this is an action on a debt, the parties are diverse (Michael is from New York and James is from New Jersey), and the amount in controversy exceeds $75,000.

The next question is whether there is a Federal Rule in the picture that potentially covers the issue before the court. Here, there is a Federal Rule in the picture, Rule 55. So the next question in the checklist is, is the federal rule or statute sufficiently broad to control the issue before the court? That is, is the Federal Rule or statute "intended or designed to govern the issue at hand" such that "the rule's purposes would be served by applying it"? Rule 55 seems to cover the situation of what a court can do when a party fails to plead or otherwise defend itself. The rule's purpose, which is presumably to require a party to present its case if it wants to resist a claim, would be furthered by its application.

Since we have a controlling Federal Rule, the *Hanna* analysis applies. The first question then is whether the Federal Rule is in direct conflict with the state statute. Here, the conflict is direct and unavoidable: The state statute expressly prohibits a default judgment under these circumstances and the Federal Rule allows it. The next question is whether the Federal Rule is constitutional. To make this determination, we inquire into whether the rule can be fairly characterized as regulating procedural matters, or if it can be classified as both procedural and substantive. The circumstances under which a court can enter judgment where a party fails to plead or defend under the rules seems to be a procedural rule and thus constitutional.

Finally, since we are dealing with a Federal Rule and not a statute, we ask whether the rule is valid under the Rules Enabling

Act. The rule certainly pertains only to the means of enforcing legal rights and thus qualifies as procedural under the Act. Next, we ask, does the Federal Rule "abridge, enlarge or modify" any substantive right? Here, it can be argued that the rule abridges the substantive protections enjoyed by New Jersey citizens against having the judicial system used as a tool for obtaining enforceable judgments on the basis of debts owed to participants in organized crime.

Given that a substantive right is arguably abridged, then we must ask whether it can be said that the Federal Rule advances clear procedural interests and only "incidentally affects litigants' substantive rights?" Clear procedural interests are advanced by the rule, as its application encourages defendants to respond to claims against them and prevents plaintiffs from having to go through the unnecessary process of litigating their claim in court against an absentee defendant. The courts certainly do not want to be bogged down with hearing cases where the defendant fails to plead or defend itself. Although it is a close call, the potentially substantive rights of defendants not to appear in actions on a debt do not seem to be merely "incidentally" affected as a byproduct of the rule but rather appear to be directly denied. The rule punishes defendants for doing something state law protects.

So, one could reasonably conclude that application of the Federal Rule in this instance would render it invalid under the Rules Enabling Act and thus inapplicable.[18] The judge would then be advised to follow the state rule barring entry of a default judgment in actions on a debt.

Here is one more problem that will demonstrate how to apply the *Erie* Doctrine checklist:

---

18. Because courts do not typically find a rule to be invalid under the Rules Enabling Act, a court might be more likely to construe the rule as not controlling of the issue in order to engage in an *Erie* analysis, which likely would favor the state rule as well (the twin aims of *Erie* would be implicated and important state policy interests would be compromised if the federal legal rule were applied).

■ PROBLEM 5.2[19] ■

New Jersey has a statute that prohibits the introduction of evidence of unconscionability in contract actions. The statute was enacted because the legislature felt that the courts had been invalidating too many contracts on the basis of claims of unconscionability, with the result that many businesses were deciding to stop doing business in New Jersey to avoid having large numbers of their contracts deemed to be unenforceable.

In federal court, judges have adopted, given the absence of any Federal Rules on the matter, the practice of allowing any evidence relevant to a contract dispute to be presented.

Little Lamb Distributors, Inc., a New York corporation based in New York, sues Mary, a New Jersey citizen, in New Jersey federal court for breach of contract for her failure to make $100,000 in payments on livestock she purchased from them. At trial, Mary offers evidence that the contract between her and Little Lamb is unconscionable.

Little Lamb objects to the introduction of this evidence, citing the New Jersey statute prohibiting such evidence. How should the court rule on the objection?

Analysis

The first question under the checklist is whether this is a diversity or federal question case. Being a suit on a contract between parties from different states for more than $75,000, it qualifies as a diversity case.

Next, we ask whether there is a federal rule in the picture that may be relevant to the issue before the court. The question does not

---

19. This question is inspired by one in GLANNON, THE GLANNON GUIDE 199–200 (2003).

disclose any relevant federal rule or statute but indicates that there is a federal judicial practice that seems to apply in the face of a conflicting state statute. Because no Federal Rule or statute is in the picture, we will have to engage in an *Erie* analysis to evaluate this Problem.

As an initial query, ask, "Can the conflicting state and federal practices be readily labeled as substantive, meaning they regulate primary rights or obligations as opposed to the form and mode of enforcing those rights or obligations?" These competing legal rules are not clearly either substantive or procedural, because they are evidentiary rules that bear on substantive protections in contract law.

Because the initial substance/procedure test does not tell us much, we next move to the modified outcome determinative test articulated in *Hanna*. Under that test, we ask whether either of the "twin aims" of *Erie* are implicated. Would application of the federal practice of allowing evidence on unconscionability impact a plaintiff's decision to file suit in federal or state court? Most certainly, because the ability of defendants to raise this issue would lead plaintiffs to prefer state court over federal court in diversity cases involving contract disputes. What about whether application of the federal practice would result in an inequitable administration of the laws? Inequities would result were the federal approach applied because non-New Jersey defendants would remove the case to federal court to avail themselves of the federal practice allowing evidence on unconscionability but New Jersey defendants would not have similar access to the federal courts and thus the federal evidentiary rule. As a result, there would be clear inequities in the administration of the laws if the federal practice were applied.

As a final check, we ask about the competing state and federal substantive policies underlying the conflicting state and federal practices. The state practice appears to be "bound up" in the state's substantive policy of the rights and obligations of parties to a contract and the goal of minimizing the number of contracts undone by the unconscionability defense. Is there a countervailing substantive federal policy underlying the federal practice? Beyond the goal of promoting a full and fair hearing of all the facts bearing on a dispute, the federal practice does not seem to have the same weighty substantive goals as the state rule. True indeed, one could argue that the federal practice is rooted in the goal of promoting justice and protecting parties' ability to raise all defenses that would help the court to do justice. But the rule seems to be more generic than that, simply permitting all relevant information without implying a grand aim of protecting the substantive rights of defendants.

Given that application of the federal practice would implicate the "twin aims" of *Erie* and the fact that the federal practice does not promote a countervailing substantive federal policy, the court should apply the state statute and sustain the objection.

POINTS TO REMEMBER

- An *Erie* analysis is necessary only for claims based on diversity jurisdiction.

- Always determine first whether there is an applicable, controlling federal rule or statute before conducting further analysis; this question determines whether an *Erie* analysis or a *Hanna* analysis is necessary.

- Federal rules and statutes are generally going to be deemed to be valid and constitutional once the *Hanna* analysis gets to that point. Thus, the critical issue typically is the determination of whether the rule or statute applies and controls the issue at hand.

- For an *Erie* analysis, take the time to go through all three analytical approaches (substance v. procedure, modified outcome-determinative test, and the *Byrd* balancing approach) when resolving a problem.

CHAPTER 6

Pleadings

Pleadings refer to the filings submitted by the parties to present their case—principally their claims and/or defenses—to the court. The pleadings generally include the complaint, the answer, and the reply.[1] Other filings, such as pre-answer motions and motions for summary judgment, are dealt with in Chapter 9.

The pleadings material, as presented in most first-year civil procedure courses, focuses on the requirements for drafting pleadings, the circumstances under which the pleadings may be amended, and the rules for ensuring that allegations made in the pleadings are truthful. This chapter will address each of these matters in turn.

REVIEW OF PLEADINGS DOCTRINE

The Complaint

Under FRCP 8(a), the plaintiff in its complaint has the burden of pleading the basis for the court's jurisdiction over the matter, a "short and plain" statement of the claim showing a right to relief, and a demand for judgment.[2] The Supreme Court has interpreted

---

1. FED. R. CIV. P. 7.

2. FED. R. CIV. P. 8(a).

Rule 8(a) as establishing a liberal "notice pleading" standard.[3] Traditionally, notice pleading has meant that the plaintiff does not have to plead detailed facts in support of its allegations in the complaint. However, recently in **Bell Atlantic Corp. v. Twombly** the Supreme Court emphasized that "a plaintiff's obligation to provide the grounds of his entitlement to relief requires more than labels and conclusions, and a formulaic recitation of the elements of a cause of action will not do."[4] For the *Twombly* Court, this meant that some facts must be pleaded, and those facts must be suggestive of liability rather than simply consistent with it.[5] Forms 11 through 21 in the Appendix of Forms to the Federal Rules provide example complaints showing what information is expected in a complaint, with Rule 84 declaring that these forms are sufficient under the Rules.

The Federal Rules depart from the general pleading standard of Rule 8(a) when it comes to certain "special matters." Rule 9(b) imposes a heightened pleading burden for allegations of fraud or mistake. The rule requires that when fraud or mistake is alleged, "a party must state with particularity the circumstances constituting fraud or mistake."[6] This particularity requirement was not meant to impose a pleading obligation significantly more burdensome than the basic pleading standard. Detailed evidence need not be pleaded; rather, sufficient information must be provided identifying the circumstances of the fraud (or mistake) such that the

---

3. Bell Atlantic Corp. v. Twombly, 127 S. Ct. 1955, 1964 (2007) ("Federal Rule of Civil Procedure 8(a)(2) requires only 'a short and plain statement of the claim showing that the pleader is entitled to relief,' in order to 'give the defendant fair notice of what the . . . claim is and the grounds upon which it rests.' ") (quoting Conley v. Gibson, 355 U.S. 41, 47 (1957)).

4. *Twombly*, 127 S. Ct. at 1964–65 (internal quotation marks omitted).

5. *Id.* at 1966 ("The need at the pleading stage for allegations plausibly suggesting (not merely consistent with) agreement reflects the threshold requirement of Rule 8(a)(2) that the 'plain statement' possess enough heft to 'sho[w]' that the pleader is entitled to relief.'").

6. Fed. R. Civ. P. 9(b). In addition to Rule 9(b)'s particularity requirement, the Private Securities Litigation Reform Act (PSLRA) offers an example of statutorily-imposed heightened pleading. *See* Private Securities Litigation Reform Act of 1995, Pub. L. No. 104–67, § 101(b), 109 Stat. 737, 747 (imposing heightened pleading standard for securities fraud class actions) (codified at 15 U.S.C. § 78u–4(b)(1)–(2)).

defendant will be able to form a response.[7] Form 21 in the Federal Rules' Appendix of Forms illustrates the fraud pleading standard and confirms that not much more detail is required under 9(b).

Rule 9 also indicates that special damages must be specifically stated in order to be claimed.[8] Special damages are those that are not the natural or inevitable result of injuries that are included in the complaint. The purpose of requiring that special damages be specifically stated is to protect opposing parties from being surprised at trial by claims of damage that would not ordinarily be the foreseeable result of the alleged events. If a court finds that a party seeking special damages did not plead those facts specifically, the party can be barred from introducing evidence on those damages at trial if the omission is deemed to be prejudicial to the opposing party.

Courts have at various times imposed heightened pleading requirements in situations not indicated in the Federal Rules as warranting such treatment. In certain disfavored or burdensome actions, such as civil rights claims, antitrust actions, suits against the government, or complex litigation, courts have imposed heightened pleading requirements in an effort to reduce the number of frivolous claims of this type that enter the system. The Supreme Court has had to intervene on several occasions to overturn such practices, indicating that it is inappropriate for lower courts to impose higher pleading requirements contrary to the notice pleading standard set out in the rules.[9] However, the Supreme Court's more recent decision in *Bell Atlantic Corp. v. Twombly* suggests that courts may indeed now be permitted to require some degree of

---

7. *See* Ziemba v. Cascade Int'l, Inc., 256 F.3d 1194, 1202 (11th Cir. 2001) ("Rule 9(b) is satisfied if the complaint sets forth (1) precisely what statements were made in what documents or oral representations or what omissions were made, and (2) the time and place of each such statement and the person responsible for making (or, in the case of omissions, not making) same, and (3) the content of such statements and the manner in which they misled the plaintiff, and (4) what the defendants obtained as a consequence of the fraud.") (citation and internal quotation marks omitted).

8. FED. R. CIV. P. 9(g).

9. *See, e.g.,* Swierkiewicz v. Sorema N.A., 534 U.S. 506 (2002); Leatherman v. Tarrant County Narcotics Intelligence & Coordination Unit, 507 U.S. 163 (1993); Conley v. Gibson, 355 U.S. 41 (1957).

factual substantiation at the pleading stage, although the Court disclaimed the notion that such a requirement rose to the level of the heightened pleading it had previously rejected.[10]

Jurisdictional allegations in complaints need only minimally allege the basis for invoking the subject matter jurisdiction of a federal court. For diversity cases, so long as the complaint indicates complete diversity of citizenship among the parties and satisfaction of the jurisdictional amount-in-controversy requirement, the requirement to plead jurisdiction is satisfied. For federal question cases, simply alleging that the case arises out of a particular federal statute, the Constitution, or a treaty will suffice. Form 7 in the Appendix to the Federal Rules of Civil Procedure provides guidance for meeting this pleading obligation.

The demand for relief required under Rule 8(a)(3) is sometimes referred to as a prayer for relief or an *ad damnum* clause when the demand is for monetary damages. Parties are not limited to the damages claimed in the prayer and may receive an award beyond what is prayed for if the evidence supports such an award.[11] However, in the case of a default judgment, the plaintiff will be limited to recovering the damages sought in the demand for relief.

Finally, it is worth noting that Rule 8(d)(2) permits a plaintiff to plead alternative or inconsistent allegations. Thus, if a plaintiff has multiple but contradictory theories of his case or versions of the facts, these may all be contained within a single complaint, keeping in mind counsel's obligations under Rule 11 (see below).

The Answer

Rule 8(b) provides for the defendant's answer to the complaint. Per Rule 12(a), the defendant generally has 20 days to respond to the complaint, either through an answer or a pre-answer motion. However, if the defendant has waived service of process pursuant to a request by the plaintiff, the defendant will have 60 days to

---

10. *Twombly*, 127 S. Ct. at 1972 ("In reaching this conclusion, we do not apply any 'heightened' pleading standard.")

11. FED. R. CIV. P. 54(c).

respond (90 days for foreign defendants). There are three types of responses to the complaint that can be contained within an answer: denials, defenses, and counterclaims. Counterclaims will be addressed in Chapter 7 on Joinder.

Under the Federal Rules, all allegations made in the complaint must be either admitted or denied; those allegations not denied (except those pertaining to the amount of damages) are deemed admitted.[12] Although general denials are permissible, such denials are only appropriate when they are sincere and truly applicable to the entirety of the paragraphs to which they apply. However, it is better practice specifically to deny or admit allegations separately. The reason for this is that if a general denial is made against a compound set of allegations, and part of those allegations are determined to be clearly true and not capable of being denied, the general denial will be ineffective and stricken, with all of the relevant allegations being deemed admitted.[13] If a party lacks information that would enable it to admit or deny a particular allegation, the Rules allow a party to plead that they are without sufficient information to form a belief as to the truth of the allegation.[14] This has the effect of a denial.

Sometimes, a denial may be so specific that it leaves open the possibility that the allegation may be true in a slightly different respect. For example, where a party denies "that they owe $100", they are leaving open the possibility that they owe a different amount. Similarly, where a party denies "doing A, B, *and* C" the party is leaving open the possibility that they did only one or two of the three things rather than all of them. The former type of denial is referred to as a *negative pregnant* and the latter as a *conjunctive denial*. Such denials may be viewed as evasive, which can result in them being deemed ineffective to deny the plaintiff's allegations. They should thus be avoided.

There are several types of defenses a party can raise in its answer to a complaint. This discussion focuses on affirmative

---

12. FED. R. CIV. P. 8(b)(6).

13. *See* Zielinski v. Philadelphia Piers, Inc., 139 F. Supp. 408 (E.D. Pa. 1956).

14. FED. R. CIV. P. 8(b)(5).

defenses; defenses available under Rule 12 are addressed in Chapter 9 on pre-trial motions. An affirmative defense is a justification or excuse that would absolve the defendant of liability to the plaintiff, even if the plaintiff's claim is proven. The defendant has the burden of proving affirmative defenses at trial and thus the Rules saddle defendants with the obligation to plead them in their answers. Although substantive law is the primary source of affirmative defenses, Rule 8(c)(1) sets out 19 affirmative defenses that must be alleged by the defendant in the answer if she intends to raise them at all. This is not an exhaustive list; Rule 8(c)(1) instructs pleaders to state "any" affirmative defense that may exist.

The failure to plead affirmative defenses can result in the defendant being barred from introducing evidence on those defenses or can lead to the waiver of those defenses.[15] The rationale behind this rule is that the defendant should not be able to ambush the plaintiff with defensive arguments that are not the natural outgrowth of the plaintiff's claim. If the plaintiff is not notified of the defendant's affirmative defenses, then the plaintiff will not be able to prepare and present its case in a way that addresses those defenses. Where no unfair surprise or prejudice to the plaintiff would result, however, the court may allow the defendant to amend its pleading to include previously not pleaded affirmative defenses and present evidence on them.

Finally, in the event that the defendant raises counterclaims in its answer, the plaintiff is entitled to an answer to respond to them.[16] The pleading rules applicable to answers ordinarily are similarly applicable to answers in response to counterclaims. Affirmative defenses must be specifically pleaded and denials must fairly meet each of the allegations made by the defendant. The Rules bar any further pleadings,[17] altering the common law practice of successive

---

15. *See, e.g.*, Ingraham v. United States, 808 F.2d 1075 (5th Cir. 1987).

16. FED. R. CIV. P. 7(a)(3). Before the Federal Rules were amended in 2007, the plaintiff's response to a counterclaim was contained in a "reply." Replies are still permitted if ordered by the court, in which a party may seek to respond to affirmative defenses or other points raised in the defendant's answer. FED. R. CIV. P. 7(a)(7).

17. FED. R. CIV. P. 7(a).

pleadings such as sur-replies. Thus, the allegations made in the final pleading are automatically deemed to be denied.[18]

Amendments

Amendments are any change to any part of a pleading (i.e., complaint, answer, and reply), and can pertain to legal issues or factual matters. Once changed, amended pleadings supersede the original pleadings. The Federal Rules allow parties to amend their pleadings once as a matter of right, so long as it is done within the prescribed time period. For amendments of pleadings to which a responsive pleading is permitted, an amendment without leave (permission) of the court or consent of the other party may be made at any time before such responsive pleading is filed.[19] If the pleading to be amended is one to which a responsive pleading is not permitted, the party has 20 days from the time of filing the pleading to amend it without leave of the court or the other party's consent.[20]

When leave of the court is required, the Rules indicate that the court should "freely give leave when justice so requires."[21] This statement provides a permissive standard for amendments but does not require the court to permit amendments in all cases. Rather, the court is to evaluate the totality of the circumstances, balancing the interests of both parties to determine whether justice would be furthered by permitting the amendment, with Rule 15(a) creating a strong presumption in favor of granting the amendment.

There are several situations where a court might decide not to permit a proposed amendment. When allowing an amendment would unfairly prejudice the adverse party—for example because the amendment is being made at a time when the adverse party would not be able to prepare an adequate response—the court has the discretion to deny leave to amend. Another possible reason to deny an amendment is that the party seeking to amend was

---

18. FED. R. CIV. P. 8(b)(6).

19. FED. R. CIV. P. 15(a).

20. *Id.*

21. *Id.*

previously aware of the information forming the basis for the amendment or failed to become aware of such information due to a lack of diligence. This is not to say that a party has a duty to exercise an onerous degree of diligence before pleading; rather, if an ordinary and expected level of investigation would have revealed the information more recently discovered, then that makes the argument in favor of permitting an amendment less strong when balanced against any unfairness or burden that the resulting amendment might place on the adverse party. Finally, if there is any indication that an eleventh-hour amendment is the result of intentional delay or bad faith, the court may deny the proposed amendment. Absent leave of the court, a party may obtain the written consent of the adverse party and thereby be permitted to amend its pleading.[22]

Rule 15(b) provides for the amendment of pleadings to conform to the evidence presented at trial. The court is to treat the pleadings as having raised issues that are tried by either the express or implied consent of the parties even though those issues were not actually raised in the pleadings. Implicit consent is likely to be found to exist if no objection is raised to the introduction of evidence having no relevance to issues raised in the pleadings. Under such circumstances, given that the evidence pertains to matters not raised in the pleadings, the parties are on notice that such new issues are being tried before the court. If an objection is made, the court is instructed to permit the amendment "freely" unless the objecting party can show prejudice.[23]

One of the most significant issues within this topic is whether an amendment will relate back to the time of the original filing of the pleading. The ability of an amendment to relate back to the time of filing becomes important where the applicable statute of limitations has expired and relation back is the only way the new allegation will be treated as if it were timely. Rule 15(c) provides for the relation back of amendments provided certain requirements are met. First, if the law providing the statute of limitations

---

22. *Id.*　　　　　　　　　　　　　　　　　**23.** Fed. R. Civ. P. 15(b).

applicable to the action permits relation back of the amendment, then it will relate back.[24] Alternatively, the amendment will relate back if the claim or defense being raised by the amendment arose out of the same "conduct, transaction or occurrence" that was set forth or "attempted to be set forth" in the original pleading.[25] Thus, when the amendment seeks to infuse claims pertaining to a different set of events than those described originally, they will not relate back under Rule 15(c)(1)(B).

If the amendment seeks to change the party against whom a claim is asserted, more stringent standards apply. The amendment will not only have to satisfy the standard set forth in Rule 15(c)(2), but two other requirements must be met. First, the party to be brought into the action via the amendment must have, within 120 days, "received such notice of the action that it will not be prejudiced in defending on the merits."[26] Second, the party to be added must have had notice that it was the intended party and "but for a mistake concerning the identity of the proper party," "the action would have been brought against it."[27] Absent such notice, or if the failure to name the party was not due to a "mistake,"[28] the amendment will not relate back to the time of filing.

Rule 11

Under Rule 11, pleadings and other papers filed with the court must be signed by counsel with the representation that the allegations and arguments that are made therein are not frivolous, have or potentially have some evidentiary support, and are not being made for an improper purpose.[29] Specifically, by signing a filing, Rule 11 indicates that counsel is representing to the court three main things. First, counsel is representing that the filing is not

---

24. Fed. R. Civ. P. 15(c)(1).

25. Fed. R. Civ. P. 15(c)(1)(B).

26. Fed. R. Civ. P. 15(c)(1)(C)(i).

27. Fed. R. Civ. P. 15(c)(1)(C)(ii).

28. *See* Worthington v. Wilson, 790 F. Supp. 829 (C.D. Ill. 1992) (denying relation back to an amendment that inserted police officers'

names as defendants where defendant had previously been styled as "three unknown named police officers" because an initial lack of knowledge is not a "mistake" under Rule 15(c)).

29. Rule 11 does not apply to discovery filings. Fed. R. Civ. P. 11(d). Such filings are governed by Rules 26(g) and 37.

being presented for an improper purpose, "such as to harass, cause unnecessary delay, or needlessly increase the cost of litigation."[30] Second, counsel is representing that the legal contentions contained in the filing are "warranted by existing law or by a nonfrivolous argument for exteding, modifying, or reversing existing law or for establishing new law."[31] Finally, counsel is representing that factual allegations or denials in the filings are supported by the evidence or are likely to have evidentiary support after further investigation.[32]

If a party believes that a paper filed with the court runs afoul of Rule 11(b), it may, by motion, ask the court to impose sanctions against opposing counsel, its law firm, and/or the adverse party. However, such a motion may not be filed with the court unless within 21 days of serving a copy of the motion on the adverse party, the challenged filing has not been withdrawn.[33] This provision is referred to as a "safe harbor" provision that gives litigants the opportunity to withdraw improper filings before being subjected to the possibility of sanctions. The court on its own may find that a filing violates Rule 11 but may only do so after giving the attorney the opportunity to demonstrate that a violation has not occurred.[34]

Sanctions for violations of Rule 11 may include non-monetary directives, monetary payments to the court or the adverse party, or the payment of reasonable attorney's fees and expenses occurring as a result of the Rule 11 violation.[35] Despite the array of sanctions, however, the court is instructed to limit sanctions for violations of Rule 11 "to what suffices to deter repetition of the conduct or comparable conduct by others similarly situated."[36] Thus, the overarching goal of the Rule 11 sanctions regime is deterrence, rather than compensation or punishment.

---

30. FED. R. CIV. P. 11(b)(1).

31. FED. R. CIV. P. 11(b)(2).

32. FED. R. CIV. P. 11(b)(3).

33. FED. R. CIV. P. 11(c)(2).

34. FED. R. CIV. P. 11(c)(3).

35. FED. R. CIV. P. 11(c)(2). Monetary damages may not be imposed for violations of Rule 11(b)(2). FED. R. CIV. P. 11(c)(5).

36. FED. R. CIV. P. 11(c)(4).

PLEADINGS CHECKLIST

With that backdrop, here is the checklist for analyzing problems presenting questions in the pleadings area:

A. ADEQUACY OF THE COMPLAINT—is the complaint (or answer setting forth counterclaims) sufficient under the Federal Rules?

    1. Jurisdiction—does the complaint adequately allege the grounds for the court's subject matter jurisdiction?

        a. **Diversity Jurisdiction**—if diversity of citizenship is alleged as the basis for jurisdiction over a claim, does the face of the complaint reveal the complete diversity of citizenship of the adverse parties in the case and satisfaction of the required amount in controversy? If so, the jurisdictional allegation is sufficient.

        b. **Federal Question Jurisdiction**—if diversity of citizenship is not alleged as the basis for jurisdiction, does the complaint allege some federal law or constitutional provision or treaty out of which the claim arises? If so, the jurisdictional allegation is sufficient.

        c. **Supplemental Jurisdiction**—if neither diversity of citizenship nor a federal question is alleged to support the jurisdiction over the claim, does the complaint allege the existence of original (diversity or federal question) jurisdiction over other claims and supplemental jurisdiction with respect to this claim? If so, the jurisdictional allegation is sufficient.

    2. Statement of the Claim—does the complaint adequately state a claim showing that the pleader is entitled to relief?

        a. **Special Matters**—does the pleading allege fraud or mistake?[37]

            i. **Yes.** If so, are the circumstances constituting fraud or mistake stated with particularity? *See* FRCP Appendix

---

37. In practice, one should also check to see whether there is a special pleading rule if the case involves an action under a federal stat- ute such as the Private Securities Litigation Reform Act (PSLRA).

Form 21 (example of fraud allegation). If not, then the pleading is insufficient. FRCP Rule 9(b).

  ii. **No.** If not, the general pleading standard of Rule 8(a)(2) applies. Proceed to the next question.

b. **All Other Claims**—does the pleading give the adverse party "fair notice of what the plaintiff's claim is and the grounds upon which it rests"? *Conley v. Gibson*, 355 U.S. 41 (1957). Ask two questions:

  i. Does the claim as pleaded, if true, entitle the plaintiff to relief under the relevant legal standard? If so, proceed to the next question.

  ii. Are sufficient facts alleged to suggest liability or is the complaint characterized by conclusory labels (e.g. he "discriminated" against me) and mere formulaic recitation of the elements of a cause of action? If facts substantiating allegations of liability are alleged, the pleading standard of Rule 8(a) has been satisfied. *Bell Atlantic Corp. v. Twombly*, 127 S. Ct. 1955 (2007).

  iii. One should also check to see whether the pleading party has tracked one of the official forms in the Appendix to the Federal Rules. If so, Rule 84 declares these Forms to satisfy the requirements of the Rules and the complaint is therefore adequate.

c. **Admissible Evidence Question**—sometimes the question you face on an exam may be phrased as, "Can a party present evidence on a particular matter, based on the pleadings?"

  i. When that is the question, answer it by first asking, "Did that party properly plead the claim as required under the Rules?"

    • **Yes.** Refer to Parts A.2.a and A.2.b above. If the matter was properly pleaded, then the party may introduce evidence pertaining to that matter.

    • **No.** If the matter was not properly pleaded as required by the Rules, proceed to the next question.

ii. **Prejudice?** Would the adverse party be unfairly prejudiced by permitting the admission of the evidence at this time?

- **Yes.** If unfair prejudice or surprise would result from the admission of the evidence on matters not properly pleaded, the evidence should be excluded.

- **No.** If no prejudice would result from admission of the evidence, the court may choose to allow the evidence to be submitted.

3. **Damages**—does the complaint adequately demand judgment for the relief the pleader seeks? An alternative form of this question may be, "Can the plaintiff recover for certain damages?" The answer to this question will depend on whether the damages were sufficiently pleaded under the Federal Rules.

a. **General Damages/Relief**—are the damages being recovered for injuries pleaded in the complaint?

i. **Yes.** If so, the complaint supports the damages award.

ii. **No.** If not, proceed to next question to determine whether the damages should be considered special damages.

b. **Special Damages**—if the damages being sought at trial are challenged as being "special damages" that should have been separately pleaded, the question becomes whether the damages at issue were indeed "special" under the rules.

i. **Natural and Foreseeable?** Are the damages the natural, foreseeable, or inevitable result of injuries or events mentioned in the complaint?

- **No.** If the damages are not natural and foreseeable but rather are unpredictable, they may be considered "special damages" and will have to be specifically stated in the pleading to be pursued. FRCP Rule 9(g).

- **Yes.** If the damages are natural and foreseeable, they should not be considered special damages and the complaint will support the recovery of the damages.

c. **Permissible Award**—beyond the adequacy of the pleading, a question may arise as to whether the party may be awarded relief beyond that prayed for in the demand for relief. To answer this question, ask, "Is relief being granted pursuant to a default judgment?"

     i. **Yes.** If so, then relief is limited to the relief prayed for in the demand for judgment. FRCP Rule 54(c).

     ii. **No.** If not, then the final judgment can grant all relief to which the party is entitled based on the evidence. Some courts may evaluate whether the adverse party would be prejudiced unfairly by allowing a recovery for a substantially different degree of relief. *See, e.g., Bail v. Cunningham Bro.*, 452 F.2d 182 (7th Cir. 1971).

B. **ADEQUACY OF THE ANSWER**—is the defendant's answer sufficient under the Federal Rules?

1. **Timeliness**—was the answer filed within the required time period under Rule 12(a)?

a. **Waiver of Service**—has the defendant waived service pursuant to a request under Rule 4(d)? If so, the defendant has 60 days to respond (90 days for foreign defendants).

b. **Service of Summons**—if the defendant was served with process, the defendant has 20 days to respond unless granted an extension by the court or through consent of the adverse party.

2. **Admissions**—are there allegations that the defendant has expressly or implicitly admitted?

a. **Express Admissions**—does the answer explicitly "admit" an allegation or set of allegations?

     i. **Yes.** If so, those allegations are admitted and the defendant cannot introduce evidence seeking to disprove those allegations unless an amendment is permitted (see Part C below).

    ii.   **No.** If not, proceed to the next question.

  b. **Implicit Admission**—are there allegations to which the defendant does not respond?

    i.   **Yes.** If so, those allegations will be deemed admitted, *see* FRCP Rule 8(b)(6), and the defendant cannot introduce evidence seeking to disprove those allegations unless an amendment is permitted (see Part C below).

    ii.   **No.** If not, and no express admission is offered, then you are dealing with a denial. Proceed to the next question to determine whether the defendant has effectively denied the allegations in question.

3. **Denials**—are the defendant's denials sufficient to deny the averments made in the complaint? If not, the defendant cannot introduce evidence seeking to disprove the ineffectively denied allegation unless an amendment is permitted (see Part C below).

  a. **General Denial**—did the defendant set forth a general denial?

    i.   **Yes.** If so, is there any portion of the allegations that were generally denied that are manifestly true or that the denying party knew was true when they denied it?

       • **Yes.** If so, the general denial will be deemed to be ineffective and the allegations will be deemed admitted. The defendant cannot introduce evidence seeking to disprove the ineffectively denied allegation unless an amendment is permitted (see Part C below).

       • **No.** If not, the general denial is effective to deny all of the allegations to which it pertains.

    ii.   **No.** If no general denial is involved, proceed to the next question.

  b. **Lack of Information**—if the answer pleads a lack of information sufficient to form a belief as to the truth or falsity of an allegation, is the matter presumptively within the defendant's knowledge?

i. **Yes.** If so, then such a response is impermissible under Rule 8(b). The response will be treated as an admission. The defendant cannot introduce evidence seeking to disprove the relevant allegation unless an amendment is permitted (see Part C below).

ii. **No.** If not, then such response is permissible under Rule 8(b). It will be treated as a denial.

c. **Negative Pregnants and Conjunctive Denials**—is the denial so specific that it leaves open the possibility of the allegation being true in a technically different respect? If so, such denials may be viewed as evasive and thus ineffective.

d. **Specific Denials**—if none of the above defects exist and specific denials are made, then the answer effectively meets the allegations of the complaint and the denied allegations will be properly placed before the finder of fact for resolution.

4. **Affirmative Defenses**—if a defendant seeks to introduce evidence pertaining to an affirmative defense, the question will be, "Has the defendant sufficiently pleaded the defense in its answer?"

a. **Affirmative Defense?** Is the defense to be treated as an affirmative defense?

i. **Rule 8(c)**—is the defense listed in Rule 8(c) as one of the affirmative defenses that must be set forth?

- **Yes.** If so, it must be set forth affirmatively in a responsive pleading.

- **No.** If not, proceed to the next question.

ii. **Substantive Law**—does the applicable substantive law define the defense as an affirmative defense?

- **Yes.** If so, it must be set forth affirmatively in a responsive pleading.

- **No.** If not, proceed to the next question.

iii. **Definitional Approach**—does the defense seek to controvert plaintiff's cause of action or provide a legal excuse or justification that absolves the defendant of liability?

- **Ordinary Defense**—if the defense merely controverts an aspect of the plaintiff's cause of action, then an ordinary defense is involved.

- **Affirmative Defense**—if the defense provides a legal excuse or justification that absolves the defendant of liability, it is an affirmative defense that must be set forth affirmatively in a responsive pleading.

- If the defense limits liability without absolving or avoiding liability altogether, some courts may consider the defense to be an affirmative defense, others may not. *Compare* **Ingraham v. United States**, 808 F.2d 1075 (5th Cir. 1987) (treating a limitation of liability as an affirmative defense), *with* **Taylor v. United States**, 821 F.2d 1428 (9th Cir. 1987) (declining to treat a limitation of liability as an affirmative defense).

   b. **Ordinary Defense**—if the defense is not classified as an affirmative defense under one of the above formulations, but rather is a defense that logically flows from plaintiff's allegations, then evidence supporting the defense is admissible under the denials provided in the answer. (Example: the defense that there is no contract in a breach of contract action is not an affirmative defense and thus need not be set forth affirmatively).

C. AMENDMENTS—is the proposed amendment proper under the Federal Rules?

   1. Amendment as a Matter of Course—is the amendment one the party is entitled to make as a "matter of course" without leave of the court under Rule 15(a)?

      a. **Response Permitted**—if a responsive pleading is permitted, then the question is, "Has the permitted responsive pleading been filed yet?"

         i. **No.** If the responsive pleading has not yet been filed, the party may amend the pleading without leave of the court.

ii. **Yes.** If the responsive pleading has been filed, then it is too late for the party to amend the pleading without leave of the court or consent of the adverse party. Proceed to Part C.2 to determine whether the amendment can be made with leave of the court.

iii. **Motions.** Motions are not considered pleadings under the Federal Rules. Thus, the filing of a preanswer motion in response to a pleading does not count as a responsive pleading for the purpose of applying Rule 15(a).

b. **Response Not Permitted**—if the pleading to be amended is one to which a responsive pleading is not permitted the question is, "Have 20 days passed since the filing of the pleading to be amended?"

i. **Yes.** If so, then it is too late to amend the pleading without leave of the court or consent of the adverse party. Proceed to Part C.2 to determine whether the amendment can be made with leave of the court.

ii. **No.** If not, the party may amend the pleading as a matter of right without the court's permission.

2. **Amendment Not as a Matter of Course**—if a party is not entitled to make the amendment as a matter of course, should the amendment be permitted?

a. **Consent**—has the adverse party consented to the amendment?

i. **Yes.** If so, the amendment should be permitted.

ii. **No.** If not, permission of the court will be required. Proceed to the next question.

b. **Leave of the Court**—should the court permit the amendment? This question is answered by asking, "Will the interests of justice be furthered by permitting the amendment?" *Yes* answers to either of the following questions raise the possibility that justice will not be served by permitting the amendment (the court could still permit the amendment in its discretion).

i. **Prejudice?** Will the adverse party be unfairly prejudiced by permitting the amendment?

ii. **Bad Faith?** Is the failure to present the information contained in the amendment earlier due to bad faith or intentional delay?

3. Amendment to Conform to Evidence—if the amendment seeks to conform a pleading to evidence presented or sought to be presented at trial, should such an amendment be permitted?

    a. **Consent**—have the parties expressly or impliedly consented to trying the issues not raised in the pleadings that are raised in the amendment?

        i. **Express Consent**—the parties may have expressly agreed to try certain issues not raised in the pleadings. If so, then the amendment is permissible.

        ii. **Implied Consent**—can consent of the parties be implied? Ask: "Was any objection raised to the introduction of evidence having no relevance to issues raised in the pleadings?"

          • **No.** If no objection was raised, that is strong evidence of implied consent.

          • **Yes.** If an objection was raised, then no consent may be implied. The court will have to resolve whether the amendment should be permitted. Proceed to the next question.

    b. **Leave of the Court**—should the court grant an amendment to conform pleadings to the evidence in the face of an objection? This question is answered by asking, "Would the objecting party be prejudiced by permitting the amendment?"

        i. **Yes.** If the objecting party would be unfairly surprised or prejudiced in its ability to maintain its action or defense, the amendment should not be permitted.

        ii. **No.** If the objecting party would not be unfairly prejudiced by permitting the amendment, then the court should permit the amendment.

D. RELATION BACK OF AMENDMENTS—if an amendment is proper and has been allowed, does it relate back to the time of filing?

1. **Statute of Limitations Law**—does the law providing the statute of limitations applicable to the action permit relation back under the circumstances? Fed. R. Civ. P. 15(c)(1)(A).

   a. **No.** If not, proceed to the next question to determine whether relation back is possible under another provision of Rule 15.

   b. **Yes.** If so, the court may permit the amendment to relate back.

2. **Amendment Involving Claim or Defense**—if the amendment involves a claim or defense, does it arise out of the same conduct, transaction, or occurrence set forth in the original pleading? Fed. R. Civ. P. 15(c)(1)(B).

   a. **No.** If the claim or defense pertains to separate events (a distinct "transaction or occurrence"), it does not relate back to the time of the original pleading.

   b. **Yes.** If the claim or defense arises out of the same transaction or occurrence, then it relates back to the time of the original pleading.

3. **Amendment Involving a New Party**—if the amendment seeks to change the party against whom a claim is asserted the answer to each of the following questions must be yes to permit the amendment to relate back. Fed. R. Civ. P. 15(c)(1)(C):

   a. **Satisfaction of Rule 15(c)(1)(B)**—are the requirements of Rule 15(c)(1)(B) satisfied? See analysis *supra* at Part D.2.

      i. **No.** If not, the amendment may not relate back.

      ii. **Yes.** If so, proceed to the next question.

   b. **Notice**—did the party to be brought into the action receive, within 120 days, notice of the institution of the action such that it will not be prejudiced in mounting a defense on the merits?

      i. **No.** If not, the amendment may not relate back.

      ii. **Yes.** If so, proceed to the next question.

   c. **Awareness of Real Party Status**—did the party to be brought into the action know that but for a mistake concerning the identity of the proper party that the action would have been brought against that party? This question can be broken down into two separate questions:

i. Did the party know (or should the party have known) that it was the intended party in the action?

- **No.** If not, the amendment may not relate back.
- **Yes.** If so, proceed to the next question.

ii. Was the failure to name the party originally due to a "mistake"?

- **No.** If not, the amendment may not relate back.
- **Yes.** The amendment relates back to the time of the filing of the original pleading.

E. **Rule 11**—are sanctions under Rule 11 appropriate in this case?

1. **Violation of Rule 11?** Has there been a violation of Rule 11?

a. **Pre-Filing Inquiry**—did the attorney or self-represented party signing the paper conduct a reasonable inquiry into the factual and legal matters presented in the filing before submitting it to the court? Fed. R. Civ. P. Rule 11(b).

i. **No.** If there was no reasonable pre-filing inquiry, a violation of Rule 11 has occurred. Proceed to Part E.2 to determine if sanctions may be imposed.

ii. **Yes.** If a reasonable pre-filing inquiry has occurred, then proceed to the next question.

b. **Improper Purpose**—has the filing been made for an improper purpose, such as harassment, delay, or to increase the cost of litigation? Fed. R. Civ. P. Rule 11(b)(1).

i. **Yes.** If there is evidence of improper purpose, a violation of Rule 11 has occurred. Proceed to Part E.2 to determine if sanctions can be imposed.

ii. **No.** If no improper purpose is evident, then proceed to the next question.

c. **Frivolous Legal Arguments**—are the legal contentions made in the filing supported by the law as it now exists or by a nonfrivolous argument "extending, modifying, or reversing existing law or for establishing new law"? Fed. R. Civ. P. Rule 11(b)(2).

i. **Existing Law**—does the filing cite to applicable law that supports the legal claims made in the filing?

- **Yes.** If so, then there is no violation of Rule 11(b)(2).

- **No.** If not, proceed to the next question.

ii. **New Law**—if the filing argues for a modification of the law, is it in an area of the law that lacks current binding precedent and based on persuasive precedent from other jurisdictions or evidence of changing legal attitudes towards existing law?

- **No.** If the argument is in an area of the law where clear, recent, and binding precedent controls the outcome, the argument for modification of the law is frivolous and in violation of Rule 11(b)(2).

- **Yes.** If the argument for modification of the law is in an area where applicable law is stale and more recent indications from other jurisdictions and from within the jurisdiction suggest support for a modification of the law, then the argument is nonfrivolous and has sufficient support to avoid running afoul of Rule 11(b)(2).

d. **Unsupportable Factual Allegations**—do the factual allegations or denials thereof have evidentiary support or, if so identified, are they likely to have evidentiary support after further investigation? Fed. R. Civ. P. Rule 11(b)(3).

i. **No.** If there is no current or prospective evidentiary support for a factual allegation or denial, then Rule 11(b)(3) or (b)(4) has been violated. Also, if it turns out that no evidentiary support develops after further investigation, further advocacy of the allegation or denial constitutes a Rule 11 violation.

ii. **Yes.** If the allegations or denials do have evidentiary support or are likely to have such support after further investigation, Rule 11 has not been violated.

2. **Sanctions**—if a violation of Rule 11 has occurred can the court impose sanctions?

a. **Motion**—has a motion for sanctions under Rule 11 been made?

    i. **Yes.** If so, have 21 days passed since the motion was served on the adverse party?

        • **Yes.** If so, has the adverse party withdrawn the challenged filing?

           – **No.** If not, then the motion may be filed with the court; the court may enter sanctions it feels would serve the goal of deterring future Rule 11 violations.

           – **Yes.** If so, then the motion may not be filed with the court and sanctions cannot be entered on the basis of the motion.

        • **No.** If 21 days have not passed, the motion cannot properly be filed with the court and sanctions thus cannot be entered on the basis of the motion.

    ii. **No.** If no motion has been made, proceed to the next question.

b. **On Court's Initiative**—has the court directed the attorney, law firm, or party to show cause to support a finding that it has not violated Rule 11(b)?

    i. **Yes.** If the court has directed the attorney, law firm, or party to show cause and the court finds that Rule 11 has been violated, it may enter sanctions if it feels that the goal of deterrence of future Rule 11 violations would be served.

    ii. **No.** If the court has not directed the attorney, law firm, or party to show cause, it may not declare a violation of Rule 11 and enter sanctions.

ILLUSTRATIVE PROBLEMS

Now, here are two problems that will enable us to see how this checklist can be used to resolve pleadings questions. They incorporate issues pertaining to the adequacy of denials, the propriety of amendments, the relation back rules, Rule 11 sanctions, the pleading of damages, and the entitlement to relief granted by a verdict:

■ PROBLEM 6.1 ■

On December 12, 2003, Johnson, a Florida citizen, brought an action against International Parcel Service (IPS), a Delaware corporation based in Georgia, in federal court in the Southern District of Florida. In paragraph 4 of his complaint, Johnson alleged, "On February 26, 2001 Marion, an IPS employee acting within the scope of employment, negligently drove a vehicle that was owned, operated, and controlled by IPS in such a manner causing it to collide with plaintiff's vehicle, causing serious injuries to the plaintiff's head, neck, and back." Paragraph 5 of the complaint sought "$750,000 in compensatory damages." Assume Florida has a three-year statute of limitations period for bringing negligence claims.

IPS responded to the complaint with an answer. In its answer, IPS responded to paragraph 4 of the complaint as follows: "IPS denies the allegations made in paragraph 4." Counsel for IPS, after reviewing the complaint had asked IPS officials about the allegations made in this paragraph and they had told him that although Marion was one of their employees, she was not driving the vehicle at the time. The vehicle in question was actually being driven by an employee of Fleet Services, the company that maintains and services IPS's fleet of vehicles. On the basis of this conversation, IPS's counsel submitted the answer containing the denial quoted above.

At trial, which commenced on March 1, 2004, after the close of Johnson's case, IPS called Marion as a witness. After counsel for IPS established that she was an employee of IPS at the time of the accident, he asked, "Were you driving the IPS vehicle involved in the accident when the accident occurred?"

Johnson's counsel immediately objects. Explain the basis for Johnson's objection to the introduction of this testimonial evidence. How should IPS's counsel respond to the objection? Are there any amendments IPS should propose? How will the judge rule on this dispute? (Be sure to discuss how the judge will rule on the objection and any amendments, and whether such amendments would relate back). Are any sanctions appropriate here?

Analysis

This Problem is essentially asking whether IPS should be permitted to present the testimony of Marion regarding whether she was driving the vehicle at the time of the accident. Why wouldn't IPS be able to present such testimony? The possibilities (given this is a pleadings, not an evidence, question) are that such evidence is relevant only to matters beyond the pleadings or directly contradicts something that has already been conclusively resolved by the pleadings. In either event, if there is a problem—from Johnson's perspective—with allowing the evidence, it must be tied to a deficiency in IPS's pleadings.

So, to determine whether there is any relevant deficiency in IPS's answer, we first ask whether IPS's denial of paragraph 4 was effective to deny each of the allegations made therein. To answer that question, the checklist directs us to see if a general denial was made. Looking at the facts from the Problem, IPS's denial simply consisted of a blanket denial of everything alleged in paragraph 4, without specifically meeting each of the individual allegations made in the paragraph. So it seems that IPS clearly entered a general denial in this case.

In the face of a general denial, the next question becomes whether any part of the allegations generally denied are manifestly true or were known to be true by the denying party at the time of the denial. Posing that question here, we find that IPS is now presenting Marion as a witness and as its employee at the time of the accident. This information is clearly inconsistent with what IPS indicated in its answer, where it denied every allegation in paragraph 4, including the allegation that Marion was an employee of IPS. (IPS's counsel is also describing the vehicle as the "IPS vehicle," possibly indicating that IPS does not deny that portion of paragraph 4 alleging IPS's ownership of the vehicle). Where it is clear that the defendant does not deny some portion of allegations that it generally denied, the general denial is treated as ineffective and the relevant allegations will be deemed admitted.

Applying that principle to this case, IPS's general denial of paragraph 4 is ineffective because of its inclusion of the allegation of Marion's status as an IPS employee, something that IPS does not deny. As a result, IPS is deemed to have admitted all of the allegations in paragraph 4. Because IPS has admitted all of the allegations in paragraph 4, IPS cannot present evidence challenging those allegations at trial unless its answer is amended to specifically admit and deny the separate allegations made in paragraph 4.

IPS's counsel should thus respond to this objection by immediately moving, under Rule 15(a), to amend their answer to admit Marion's employee status and ownership of the IPS vehicle but specifically deny the remainder of paragraph 4. Under Rule 15(a) amendments are to be "freely" permitted if the interests of justice would be furthered. To determine whether justice would be served by permitting an amendment in this case, the checklist directs us to ask whether there is any indication of bad faith or prejudice to the adverse party. There is no indication of bad faith or intent to delay here; rather, the initial denial appears to have been a result of counsel's sloppiness in not parsing the separate allegations made in paragraph 4 that it intended to deny. Regarding prejudice to Johnson, if IPS is permitted to amend its answer Johnson may not be able to establish IPS's liability. Neither would Johnson be able to bring an action against the seemingly more appropriate party, Fleet Services, because the applicable statute of limitations period has expired. So it does appear that a good degree of prejudice would result if the amendment were granted. That suggests that the court should not allow the amendment.

However, IPS's counsel can argue that Johnson can amend his complaint to substitute Fleet Services as a party and that such an amendment will relate back to the time of filing under Rule 15(c), permitting Johnson to proceed against the proper party. Would such an amendment be granted and if so would it relate back? The amendment would likely be granted, since there is no bad faith on the part of Johnson and no prejudice to IPS would result (in fact, IPS would benefit from the amendment).

Regarding relation back, because the amendment would be attempting to change the party against whom a claim is asserted, it would only relate back if a series of questions can be given affirmative responses. First, would the amendment satisfy Rule 15(c)(1)(B), meaning that the amended claim arose out of the same transaction or occurrence set forth in the original pleading? The answer here is yes, since the allegations against Fleet Services arise out of the same accident. Second, did Fleet Services receive, within 120 days of filing, notice that the action commenced and notice that but for a mistake it would have been the party sued? The facts do not give any indication that IPS communicated the commencement of this action to Fleet Services; so, based on the facts, it appears that Fleet Services has not received any notice of this lawsuit. Thus, an amendment to Fleet Services would not relate back to the time of filing of the complaint.

In sum, because Johnson does not have an available means of bringing an action against Fleet Services, either via an amendment or commencing a new action, he would be unfairly prejudiced by permitting IPS to amend its pleadings to deny allegations previously admitted. The court should therefore deny IPS's motion to amend and sustain Johnson's objection to the introduction of evidence seeking to disprove the allegations made in paragraph 4.

Regarding the propriety of sanctions, it does not appear that any sanctions are warranted here. IPS's counsel generally denied paragraph 4, which was not warranted by the evidence at IPS's disposal since Marion was known to be an employee. That appears to be a violation of Rule 11(b)(4). Johnson has not moved for sanctions so any sanctions would have to be on the court's own initiative. However, sanctions do not appear appropriate at this time because the general denial has been deemed ineffective and treated as an admission, itself a sanction that benefits Johnson. Because there no longer appears to be any offending filing in violation of Rule 11, no further deterrent purpose would be served by the imposition of Rule 11 sanctions. The court should thus not impose sanctions against IPS.

***

■ PROBLEM 6.2 ■

***

Same facts as above. At the trial, while Johnson was testifying as a witness, he testified that his physical injuries have resulted in great physical pain and suffering that have not gone away. His attorney then went on to ask him about any mental anguish that he is suffering as a result of the accident. IPS's counsel objects to the question about mental anguish because it goes to special damages not pleaded in the complaint. The objection is overruled.

At the conclusion of the trial, the jury returns a verdict for Johnson, awarding him $1 million for his physical injuries and pain and suffering and an additional $1 million for his mental anguish. Counsel for IPS immediately moves to have the verdict for mental anguish vacated and for the $1 million for physical injuries remitted down to the $750,000 figure pleaded in Johnson's complaint.

Was the court correct to overrule IPS's objection to the introduction of mental anguish testimony? How should the court rule on IPS's motion to reduce the award?

Analysis

***

The first question asks us to determine whether IPS's objection to mental anguish testimony should have been sustained. The Problem indicates that IPS was objecting on the grounds that mental anguish arising out of this accident constitutes special damages that were not pleaded in the complaint. So, to determine whether the objection should have been sustained, we must ask whether Johnson adequately pleaded mental anguish. Looking to Johnson's complaint, it alleges "serious injuries to the plaintiff's head, neck, and back" as a result of a motor vehicle accident. There is no indication in the complaint that there were injuries to other parts of plaintiff's body and no indication that there was any damage to the plaintiff's mental state. Thus, the complaint does not plead mental anguish as damages.

Because mental anguish is not pleaded in the complaint, the checklist directs us next to ask whether mental anguish should be considered special damages that must be specifically pleaded. Is mental anguish the natural, foreseeable, or inevitable result of the injuries or events alleged in Johnson's complaint? Although a certain amount of mental anguish is sometimes possible as a result of a motor vehicle accident, it does not always and necessarily result from such an accident. Similarly, although mental anguish can arise out of suffering physical injuries to one's head, neck, and back, mental anguish does not always or inevitably result from such injuries. Given these facts, plus the fact that Johnson expressly listed his specific injuries, which indicates the exclusion of other injuries not mentioned, the court should have concluded that mental anguish did constitute special damages. Because mental anguish constitutes special damages that were not specifically stated in the complaint, Johnson should not have been allowed to present evidence relevant to such damages and the court should have sustained IPS's objection.

Now IPS is objecting to the jury verdict and seeking a remittitur to $750,000. The jury verdict can be broken down into two separate components: $1 million in compensatory damages for physical injuries and pain and suffering and $1 million for mental anguish. Regarding the award for mental anguish, under Rule 54(c) the award is permissible if it is supported by the evidence even though it goes beyond the amount sought in the demand for judgment. Here, evidence of mental anguish was admitted, over IPS's objection, and thus the jury apparently had some basis for its award. If the court were inclined to reconsider its earlier decision to allow the evidence in light of the fact that mental anguish indeed constitutes special damages in this case, then the court could grant IPS's motion and vacate the $1 million verdict for mental anguish.

However, if the court stands by its earlier evidentiary ruling, the jury award will have support and its mental anguish verdict should be upheld under Rule 54(c).

Regarding the $1 million verdict for physical injuries and pain and suffering, so long as the evidence supports a $1 million award, the jury is entitled to give it, notwithstanding the fact that Johnson's complaint only sought $750,000. The Problem indicates that testimony regarding physical pain and suffering showed that Johnson endures "great physical pain and suffering" and that such pain has endured for over three years and continues to this day. That testimony could support the jury's conclusion that Johnson was entitled to more compensation than he sought. Under Rule 54(c), the jury is permitted to award a greater amount in such circumstances. Thus, the court should reject IPS's motion to remit the $1 million verdict for physical injuries to $750,000.

POINTS TO REMEMBER

- Resolving pleadings problems will require the use of legal judgment. There are not many black and white rules in this area; rather, the Rules set forth standards that require assessments of justice and a balancing of the parties' interests. Weigh the issues on each side and reach a reasoned result based on your own judgment that you can defend.

- Think about the pleadings material not simply from the perspective of the party making the pleading, but from the perspective of the opponent. These rules are not just a "how to" of pleading; they provide rules that, if not followed, can prevent admissibility of evidence if objected to by the opponent.

- Always be on the lookout for ineffective responses to allegations. If ineffective responses or no responses are present, admissions will result, which will have implications for the admissibility of evidence. Admitted allegations cannot be contested at trial absent an amendment.

- Look at the pleadings requirements and amendment requirements as going hand-in-hand. If a pleading turns out to be deficient in some respect, immediately ask whether an amendment can be permitted to cure the deficiency.

- Remember that amendments can be made at any time, not just before trial; they can be made during and after the trial, so long as the rules for permitting amendments are satisfied.

- The Federal Rules heavily favor the granting of amendments in order to further the goal of resolving disputes on the merits. Thus, the degree of prejudice warranting the denial of an amendment must be substantial and unfair.

- Do not forget about the safe-harbor provision when considering the propriety of sanctions under Rule 11. The court cannot grant a motion for sanctions under Rule 11 if the party making the motion has not served the adverse party with the motion 21 days prior to submitting it with the court and provided the challenged filing has not been corrected or withdrawn.

*

CHAPTER 7

Joinder of Claims and Parties

Joinder of claims and parties involves the addition of claims and parties beyond the basic lawsuit that contains only a single plaintiff with one claim against a single defendant. Moving beyond that simple structure is facilitated in the Federal Rules by a collection of rules that authorize but also limit the extent to which various parties may bring or add claims within a single action against existing parties or new parties. The rules also provide for claims by non-parties to be asserted against those who are already parties in an action. This chapter will review all of these rules but will not touch on the subject of class actions, a complex joinder issue not addressed in this book.

REVIEW OF CLAIM JOINDER

Basic Claim Joinder

Basic claim joinder refers to the process of joining multiple claims against an opposing party in one action. Rule 18, which governs claim joinder, provides that a party asserting a claim may join as many claims of any kind as the party has against an opposing party.[1] This right applies to parties making original claims, counterclaims, crossclaims, or third-party claims.[2] This rule provides no limitation on the number or type of claims that a party may join to its original claim. However, a claimant must first successfully assert a claim against a party under one of the rules before it will be able to join other claims against that same party. Further, a court may decide claims joined under Rule 18(a) only if the joined claims independently satisfy the subject matter jurisdiction and venue requirements.[3] Importantly, though, the decision to join additional unrelated claims under Rule 18(a) is discretionary; thus a party failing to join such claims is free to raise those claims in a subsequent action. Closely related claims, however, might have to be raised concurrently at the risk of being barred under the doctrine of claim preclusion in any future actions.[4]

Counterclaims

Counterclaims are claims made by defending parties against parties who bring claims against them. For example, if *A* brings a claim against *B*, and *B* has a claim it asserts against *A*, *B*'s claim against *A* within this action would be called a counterclaim. Counterclaims are governed by Rule 13, which classifies counterclaims as either compulsory or permissive.

A compulsory counterclaim, which is governed by Rule 13(a), is a claim that a defending party has that arises out of the same transaction or occurrence that is the subject matter of the opposing party's claim. Such counterclaims must be asserted by a party or that party waives the right to assert that claim against the opposing party in the future and is barred or estopped from asserting it in any subsequent action.[5] Permissive counterclaims, which are gov-

---

1. FED. R. CIV. P. 18(a).

2. *Id.*

3. King Fisher Marine Serv., Inc. v. 21st Phoenix Corp., 893 F.2d 1155, 1158 n.2 (10th Cir. 1990). The requirement that joined claims independently satisfy the subject matter jurisdiction and venue requirements is a product of Rule 82, which provides that the Federal Rules "do not extend or limit

the jurisdiction of the district courts or the venue of actions in those courts." FED. R. CIV. P. 82.

4. See Chapter 11 for a discussion of preclusion doctrine.

5. Such claims may not be raised as counterclaims if they would require the presence of third parties over whom the court cannot acquire personal jurisdiction. FED. R. CIV. P.

erned by Rule 13(b), are simply those claims a defending party has against an opponent that do not arise out of the same transaction or occurrence. Such claims may be raised by the party but need not be.

Like claim joinder under Rule 18(a), there is no limitation to the type or number of counterclaims a party may bring under Rule 13. However, also like claims joined under Rule 18(a), counterclaims must independently satisfy jurisdictional and venue requirements. Because compulsory counterclaims arise out of the same transaction or occurrence as the claim asserted by the opposing party, there will generally be supplemental jurisdiction over such claims in the event that they lack an independent basis for federal jurisdiction, provided the provisions of paragraph (b) of the supplemental jurisdiction statute do not operate to deny supplemental jurisdiction under the circumstances.[6] Permissive counterclaims, on the other hand, are less likely to qualify for supplemental jurisdiction, although it is possible for claims not arising out of the same transaction or occurrence to satisfy the common nucleus of operative fact standard of supplemental jurisdiction.[7]

Determining whether a counterclaim arises out of the same transaction or occurrence as the claim asserted by an opposing party is typically done with reference to the so-called "logical relationship" test, which holds that claims that are logically related to one another satisfy the transaction or occurrence standard. A logical relationship, in turn, exists when the claims are offshoots of the same basic controversy between the parties or otherwise related in such a way that separate trials on each of the claims would involve "a substantial duplication of effort and time by the parties

---

13(a). This facet of the compulsory counterclaim rule is typically not discussed or tested in the basic first-year civil procedure course.

6. *See* 28 U.S.C. § 1367(b).

7. Jones v. Ford Motor Credit, 358 F.3d 205, 213 (2d Cir. 2004) (concluding that permissive counterclaims may be able to qualify for supplemental jurisdiction under 28 U.S.C. § 1367); Rothman v. Emory Univ., 123 F.3d 446, 454 (7th Cir. 1997) (suggesting that the "case or controversy" test under § 1367 is broader than the logical relationship test that is applied to compulsory counterclaims).

and the courts" or the presentation of similar bodies of evidence.[8] Courts have not consistently applied the logical relationship test in a way that provides clear guidance for students of civil procedure. However, although the logical relationship standard does not provide a bright-line rule for evaluating whether claims arise out of the same transaction or occurrence, remembering the policy underlying the standard will help: courts are interested in achieving an efficient use of judicial resources, minimizing the burden imposed on litigants, and avoiding unnecessary impositions on testifying witnesses. When it appears that not hearing the two claims together will undermine these goals by resulting in duplicative litigation, then it is more likely that a logical relationship between the claims exists.

Crossclaims

A crossclaim is a claim brought by one coparty against another coparty. For example, if A brings a claim against B and C, and B has a claim against C, B's claim against C within this action is referred to as a crossclaim. Crossclaims are governed by Rule 13(g) and, like compulsory counterclaims, they must arise out of the same transaction or occurrence that is the subject matter of the original action or of a counterclaim that has been asserted. Crossclaims may also assert contingent or derivative claims for liability on claims against the crossclaimant. Also like compulsory counterclaims, because crossclaims are transactionally related to claims over which the court has subject matter jurisdiction, crossclaims will generally satisfy the requirements of supplemental jurisdiction.[9]

However, unlike compulsory counterclaims, crossclaims do not have to be asserted and are thus permissive; a party may opt not to assert a crossclaim without fear of forfeiting the claim. The only wrinkle in this formulation is that once a coparty asserts a crossclaim against another coparty, the latter party is placed in an

---

8. Great Lakes Rubber Corp. v. Herbert Cooper Co., 286 F.2d 631 (3d Cir. 1961).

9. This statement is made with the caveat that the language of 28 U.S.C. § 1367(b) should always be consulted to determine whether circumstances warrant the denial of supplemental jurisdiction.

adversarial relationship with the crossclaimant; thus, the party against whom a crossclaim is asserted must assert all transactionally related claims available as compulsory counterclaims under Rule 13(a) or they will be waived. Beyond that issue, questions involving crossclaims will involve the same central issue involved with compulsory counterclaims: whether the crossclaim arises out of the same transaction or occurrence as the principal claim or a counterclaim. This determination is made with reference to the same logical relationship test used to evaluate counterclaims.

REVIEW OF PARTY JOINDER

Permissive Party Joinder

Moving from the addition of claims to the addition of parties adds another layer of complexity to lawsuits that understandably can be confusing for students. Rule 20 speaks to the permissive joinder of parties in a single action. Under Rule 20, plaintiffs may join together in one action if they assert claims arising out of the same transaction or occurrence involving common questions of law or fact.[10] Similarly, parties may be joined together as defendants (they are so joined by the plaintiffs asserting claims against them) where the claims brought against them arise out of same transaction or occurrence and involve common questions of law or fact.[11] Whether claims arise out of the same transaction or occurrence is determined by application of the logical relationship test used to assess the status and propriety of counterclaims and crossclaims. However, in addition to having some logical relationship with one another, the claims must share at least one common question of fact or a common legal question. Claims arising from the same transaction or occurrence typically will satisfy this latter requirement, although it is possible under some formulations of the logical relationship test for claims to be logically related to one another but not have any factual or legal questions in common.[12] If both

---

10. Fed. R. Civ. P. 20(a).

11. *Id.*

12. *See, e.g.*, United States v. Heyward–Robinson Co., 430 F.2d 1077 (2d Cir. 1970).

(finding that two separate contract disputes between the same parties were logically related to one another, even though no common questions of law or fact existed).

requirements laid out in Rule 20 are satisfied, the parties may be joined. However, the requirements of personal jurisdiction, subject matter jurisdiction, and venue will have to be satisfied with respect to such parties and the claims associated with them.

Compulsory Party Joinder

Compulsory party joinder is a more difficult issue. Under Rule 19, certain persons not party to an action must be joined to the action, if feasible, in order for the court to be able to render a just resolution of the action before it. Persons to be joined if feasible—so-called "necessary parties"—are those who fit into one of three categories presented in the Rule.

First, a person is a necessary party if in the person's absence complete relief cannot be accorded among the existing parties. For example, assume *A* sues *B* to recover property he sold to *B* and *C* on the ground of misrepresentation. Because *C* is a co-owner of the property, if *C* is not joined, *A* will not be able to recover the property without initiating a second action against *C*. *A* thus cannot obtain complete relief solely in its action against *B*. *C* would be a necessary party in this example.

Second, a person is a necessary party if the person claims an interest relating to the subject of the action and disposition of the action in the person's absence may impair or impede that person's ability to protect that interest. For example, assume *A* sues *B* seeking payment of money from a limited fund. If *C* is similarly entitled to payment from that fund, but a judgment in *A v. B* would deplete the fund, *C*'s future ability to collect on its claim would be impaired. *C* could thus be considered a necessary party.[13]

Finally, a person is considered a necessary party if the person claims an interest relating to the subject of the action and disposition of the action in the person's absence would leave existing parties subject to a substantial risk of incurring double, multiple, or otherwise inconsistent obligations by reason of the claimed interest.

---

13. *See, e.g.,* United States v. Bank of N.Y. & Trust Co., 296 U.S. 463, 480 (1936).

For example, assume A sues B for possession of land. B leases the land from C. If A prevails in the action against B, B will lose possession of the land but will still be obligated to pay rent to C. Thus, C should be treated as a necessary party to avoid the possibility that B would be subjected to two inconsistent obligations in this situation.[14]

An example of a party who would not be considered to be necessary under Rule 19 would be a joint tortfeasor. That is, in a situation where A (the patient) alleges negligence against B (the manufacturer of an allegedly defective medical device), C (the doctor), and D (the hospital), where each was involved in the operation installing the device in A, all the defendants would be considered joint tortfeasors that need not be joined under Rule 19.[15] The Supreme Court has held, based in part on the Advisory Committee's note to Rule 19, that joint tortfeasors are simply permissive parties and thus do not qualify as necessary parties under Rule 19(a).[16]

What are the consequences of being determined to be a necessary party under Rule 19(a)? Under the Rule, all such parties must be joined in the action if feasible. Such joinder is mandatory and parties who refuse to join the action will be declared to be a party and the results of the action will be binding against them.

Under what circumstances will joinder not be feasible? Three situations come to mind. First, if the court cannot obtain personal jurisdiction over the party to be joined under Rule 19, joinder will not be feasible.[17] Second, if there would be no subject matter jurisdiction over the claims asserted by or against the Rule 19 party—typically because the joinder of the party would destroy diversity—then the joinder would not be feasible. Finally, if the

---

14. *See, e.g.*, Washington v. United States, 87 F.2d 421, 431 (9th Cir. 1936).

15. *See* Temple v. Synthes Corp., 498 U.S. 5, 8 (1990).

16. *See id.* ("The Advisory Committee Notes to Rule 19(a) explicitly state that 'a tortfeasor with the usual joint-and-several liability is merely a permissive party to an action against another with like liability.' ").

17. Rule 4(k)(1)(B) provides federal courts with the ability to serve (and thereby obtain jurisdiction over) Rule 19 parties within 100 miles of the courthouse where the action is pending.

court would lack venue over the claims pertaining to the party to be joined, joinder would not be feasible, provided the prospective party objects to venue.

Under certain circumstances, courts are able to declare that the inability to join a necessary party is of sufficient concern to prevent the court from proceeding with the action at all in that party's absence; such parties are referred to as being "indispensable."[18] Making such a determination depends on how a court evaluates four factors outlined in Rule 19(b):

1. The extent to which a judgment rendered in the person's absence might be prejudicial to the person or those already parties;

2. The extent to which, by protective provisions in the judgment the prejudice can be lessened or avoided;[19]

3. Whether a judgment rendered in the person's absence will be adequate; and

4. Whether the plaintiff will have an adequate remedy if the action is dismissed for non-joinder.

These factors must be applied to the specific facts of a case with "equity and good conscience"; a determination that a party is indispensable but cannot feasibly be joined results in the dismissal of the case.[20]

Third-Party Practice (Impleader)

Under Rule 14(a) a defending party can assert a claim against a nonparty (the "third-party") claiming that the third party is liable to the defending party (now the "third-party plaintiff") for all or

---

18. Fed. R. Civ. P. 19(b).

19. For example, if protective provisions may be inserted in the judgment that would protect the absent party's interest, that suggests that the necessary party may not be considered indispensable and the court could keep the case without prejudicing the outsider.

20. See *Shimkin v. Tompkins, McGuire, Wachenfeld & Barry*, No. 02 Civ. 9731, 2003 WL 21964959, at *1 (S.D.N.Y. Aug. 19, 2003), for an example of a Rule 19(b) analysis and a dismissal for failure to join an indispensable party.

part of the claim being asserted against that defending party. For example, if *A* sues *B* and *B* feels that *C* should be liable to *B* if *B* is liable to *A*, *B* can bring such a claim against *C*, impleading *C* into the action as a third-party defendant. The Rule provides that such claims against third parties can only be for reimbursement for all or part of any amount a defending party would owe to its opponent if the opponent prevails. Thus, a defending party cannot simply implead a third-party for a related claim, even if it arises out of the same transaction and occurrence. However, once a third-party claim is properly asserted, the third-party plaintiff may join additional claims against the third-party defendant under Rule 18(a). Claims that may be brought as claims against third parties are permissive only and may be brought at the defending party's option.

The court must be able to obtain personal jurisdiction against the third-party in order for the third-party to be joined.[21] Also, subject matter jurisdiction must exist over claims against third-parties. The supplemental jurisdiction statute explicitly provides that claims involving the joinder of additional parties are included in the jurisdictional grant of the statute.[22] A claim against a third-party is such a claim and generally will qualify for supplemental jurisdiction. However, state-law claims by plaintiffs in diversity actions against nondiverse third-party defendants will not qualify for supplemental jurisdiction under the terms of the statute.[23] Finally, venue requirements appear not to be an issue for claims surrounding the third-party defendant, provided venue is properly established for the original action.[24]

A defending party may assert claims against third parties without the permission of the court within 10 days of service of its answer or anytime thereafter with leave of the court. Leave will be

---

21. As is the case for Rule 19 parties, Rule 4(k)(1)(B) expands the reach of federal courts against Rule 14 third parties by permitting service to be effective within a 100–mile radius from the courthouse ("100–mile Bulge Rule").

22. 28 U.S.C. § 1367(a).

23. 28 U.S.C. § 1367(b).

24. 6 Wright & Miller, FEDERAL PRACTICE AND PROCEDURE § 1445.

denied generally if inclusion of the third party would result in undue delay or prejudice to the plaintiff.

Third-party defendants are themselves permitted to assert claims. A third-party defendant may assert counterclaims against the party impleading it into the action (the third-party plaintiff) or crossclaims against other third-party defendants. A third-party defendant may also assert against a plaintiff any claims arising from the same transaction and occurrence giving rise to the plaintiff's claim. In the event that the plaintiff brings a claim against a third-party defendant, the third-party defendant and the plaintiff would become opposing parties under Rule 13. As such, the third-party defendant would have to bring any compulsory counterclaims it had against that plaintiff or they would be waived.

As already alluded to, a plaintiff may assert any claims against a third-party defendant, but only those arising from same transaction and occurrence as the plaintiff's claim against the defendant/third-party plaintiff.[25] If the third-party defendant asserts a claim against a plaintiff, the plaintiff will be governed by Rule 13 regarding counterclaims against the third-party defendant and must bring any compulsory counterclaims or waive them.

Intervention

Intervention involves a nonparty intervening in an action and making themselves a party. Rule 24 governs intervention and provides both for "Intervention of Right" and "Permissive Intervention." Under Rule 24(a)(2), a nonparty has a right to intervene in an action when (1) it claims an interest in the subject of the action, (2) the nonparty is so situated that disposition of the action would impair its ability to protect that interest, and (3) the nonparty's interest is not adequately represented by existing parties in the action.[26]

If there is an existing party in the action who has a similar stake in the outcome of the action as the absentee, and that party is

---

25. Rule 18(a) will permit the plaintiff to join additional claims once she successfully asserts a transactionally related claim against the third-party defendant.

26. Fed. R. Civ. P. 24(a)(2).

not in collusion with the opposing party, the right to intervene will generally be denied because the absentee's interest will be deemed to be adequately represented.[27]

Rule 24(a) also requires a "timely" application to intervene. There is no fixed time limit for seeking intervention and it can be done at any time. However, timeliness will be assessed with reference to whether the parties and the court will suffer from the fact that the application did not come earlier and whether the applicant can be faulted for seeking to intervene at a late stage in the process.[28]

Rule 24(b) speaks to permissive intervention. Under this rule, intervention "may" be permitted when the absentee's claim or defense shares a question of law or fact with the main action.[29] The policy underlying permissive intervention is simply to promote judicial economy; no threatened impairment of the intervenor's interest is at issue here. Thus, courts balance the interest in efficient resolution of disputes against the complexity and other costs that might result from adding the intervenor.[30]

As with other joinder provisions, the ability to intervene under Rule 24 does not ensure that the court will be able to hear the claim. Claims asserted by intervenors must independently qualify for subject matter jurisdiction and satisfy federal venue requirements. If no independent basis for subject matter jurisdiction exists, supplemental jurisdiction will not be available in diversity-only actions for state-law claims asserted by parties seeking to intervene under Rule 24.[31]

Finally, although the ability to intervene may be "of right" or "permissive," it is important to recognize that both forms of intervention are permissive in the sense that the intervenor has the discretion to decide whether to intervene. There is no such thing as

27. Gene R. Shreve & Peter Raven–Hansen, Understanding Civil Procedure 280 (3d ed. 2002).

28. See id. at 280–81.

29. Fed. R. Civ. P. 24(b)(1)(B).

30. See id. at 281.

31. 28 U.S.C. § 1367(b).

a compulsory intervention under Rule 24 (although a party could be compulsorily joined under Rule 19).

JOINDER CHECKLIST

With that backdrop, here is the checklist for analyzing problems presenting questions involving claim and party joinder:

A. **PERMISSIBILITY OF THE CLAIM.** Is the joinder of the claim permitted under the Rules? ***Note:*** *this analysis only determines whether the claim can be pleaded. A separate analysis is necessary to determine whether the court will have subject matter jurisdiction to hear the case and venue.*[32]

1. **Defending Party's Claim against Opposing Party**—is the claim in question being asserted against a party who has asserted a claim against the claimant? ·

    a. **No.** If not, proceed to Part A.2.

    b. **Yes.** If so, the claim may be asserted as a counterclaim. Next ask whether the claim arises out of the same transaction or occurrence as the claim asserted against the counterclaimant. This question is answered with reference to the logical relationship test: is there a logical relationship between the claims? Will requiring separate trials result in duplicative multiple litigation?

        i. **Yes.** If the claims arise out of the same transaction or occurrence, the counterclaim is *compulsory* and must be asserted or it will be waived.[33]

        ii. **No.** If the claims do not arise out of the same transaction and occurrence, the counterclaim is merely *permissive* and may be brought at the counterclaimant's option.

---

32. These topics are addressed in Chapters 3 and 4, respectively.

33. This statement is made with the caveat that if adjudication of such a counterclaim would require the presence of third parties over whom the court cannot acquire jurisdiction, the counterclaim cannot be brought. FED. R. CIV. P. 13(a).

2. Claim against Non–Aggressor[34]—if the claim is not being made against an opposing party asserting a claim against the claimant, against whom is the claim being asserted?

    a. **An Opposing Party Defendant**—if the claim at issue is being asserted against an opposing party defendant, the claim may be joined with the claimant's original or existing claim under Rule 18(a).

    b. **Coparty**—if the claim is being asserted against a coparty (a party aligned on the same side of the "v."), does the claim arise out of the same transaction or occurrence as the subject matter of the original claim or a counterclaim therein or assert that the party against whom it is asserted is or may be liable to the claimant for all or part of a claim against the claimant?

        i. **Yes.** If so, the claim may (not must) be asserted as a crossclaim under Rule 13(g).

        ii. **No.** If not, the claim may not be asserted as a crossclaim unless the claimant has already successfully asserted a claim against the coparty, in which case the claim at issue could be joined to that existing claim under Rule 18(a).

    c. **Rule 14 Party**—if the claim is against an existing third-party defendant, what is the party status of the claimant?

        i. **Third-party Plaintiff**—if the claimant is the third-party plaintiff, the claim at issue can be joined to the existing third-party claim under Rule 18(a).

        ii. **Plaintiff**—if the claimant is the plaintiff, does their claim against the third-party defendant arise out of the same transaction or occurrence as the plaintiff's claim against the third-party plaintiff?

            • **Yes.** If so, the claim may (not must) be asserted against the third-party defendant.

            • **No.** If not, the claim is not permitted under Rule 14(a). However, if the plaintiff has already suc-

---

34. This term refers to a party who has not asserted a claim against the claimant.

cessfully asserted a claim against the third-party
defendant, the claim at issue can be joined to
that existing claim under Rule 18(a).

    iii. **Coparty**—if the claimant is a coparty of the third-
party defendant, conduct analysis at *supra* Part A.2.b.

  d. **The Plaintiff by a Third–Party Defendant**—if the claim is
by a third-party defendant against the plaintiff, does the
claim arise out of the same transaction or occurrence as
the plaintiff's claim against the third-party plaintiff?

    i. **Yes.** If so, the claim may (not must) be asserted against
the plaintiff.

    ii. **No.** If not, the claim is not permitted under Rule
14(a). However, if the third-party defendant has already successfully asserted a claim against the plaintiff,
the claim at issue can be joined to that existing claim
under Rule 18(a).

  e. **Rule 19 or 24 Party**—the permissibility of claims against
such parties depends on their status in the lawsuit once
joined. Determine which of the above-mentioned party-
classifications properly describes the position of the party
in the action and apply that analysis.

B. **PERMISSIVE PARTY JOINDER.** Is the joinder of a party permissible?

  1. **Joinder of Defendants**—is the plaintiff asserting against the
defendants a right to relief arising out of the same transaction
or occurrence and involving a common question of law or
fact?

    a. **Yes.** If so, the plaintiff may join the defendants in a single
action under Rule 20(a).

    b. **No.** If not, the plaintiff may not join the defendants
together in a single action.

  2. **Joinder of Plaintiffs**—are the plaintiffs asserting a right to
relief arising out of the same transaction or occurrence and
involving a common question of law or fact?

    a. **Yes.** If so, the plaintiffs may join together in a single action
under Rule 20(a).

b. **No.** If not, the plaintiffs may not join together in a single action.

3. **Joinder of Nonparties**—is the party seeking joinder a defending party?

   a. **No.** If not, the party may not implead a nonparty into the action as a third-party defendant under Rule 14(a). Proceed to Part C to determine whether the party can seek compulsory joinder of the party through Rule 19.

   b. **Yes.** If so, is the party seeking to assert against the nonparty a claim that the nonparty is liable to the impleading party for all or part of the plaintiff's claim against the defending party?

      i. **Yes.** If so, the claim is a proper and can properly be asserted against the nonparty. The nonparty becomes a third-party defendant.

      ii. **No.** If not, the party will not be able to implead the nonparty into the action as a third-party defendant.

4. **Joinder by Nonparties**—if the party seeking joinder is a nonparty, do they have a right to intervene under Rule 24(a)(2)?

   a. **Interest in Action.** Does the nonparty have an interest in the subject of the action?

      i. **No.** If not, the nonparty has no right to intervene under Rule 24(a)(2). Proceed to Part B.4.d to determine whether their intervention is permissible.

      ii. **Yes.** If so, proceed to the next question.

   b. **Impairment to Interest.** Would disposition of the action impair the nonparty's ability to protect its interest?

      i. **No.** If not, the nonparty has no right to intervene under Rule 24(a)(2). Proceed to Part B.4.d to determine whether their intervention is permissible.

      ii. **Yes.** If so, proceed to the next question.

   c. **Adequate Representation of Interest.** Is the nonparty's interest adequately represented by existing parties?

i. **Yes.** If so, the nonparty has no right to intervene under Rule 24(a)(2). Proceed to Part B.4.d to determine whether their intervention is permissible.

ii. **No.** If not, and the previous questions have been answered affirmatively, the nonparty has a right to intervene under Rule 24(a)(2).

d. **Permissive Intervention**—do the nonparty's claim or defense and the main action have a question of law or fact in common?

i. **Yes.** If so, then the nonparty may be permitted to intervene in the discretion of the court under Rule 24(b).

ii. **No.** If not, the nonparty is not permitted to intervene.

C. **COMPULSORY PARTY JOINDER.** Must a nonparty be joined in an action?

1. **Necessary Party Status.** Is the absentee a necessary party under Rule 19(a)?

a. **Availability of Complete Relief**—in the nonparty's absence, is the court able to afford complete relief among those who are already parties to the action?

i. **No.** If not, the nonparty is a necessary party. Proceed to the feasibility analysis.

ii. **Yes.** If so, proceed to the next question.

b. **Impairment to Absentee's Claimed Interest**—would disposition of the action in the nonparty's absence impair or impede the nonparty's ability to protect their claimed interest relating to the subject of the action?

i. **Yes.** If so, the nonparty is a necessary party. Proceed to the feasibility analysis.

ii. **No.** If not, then proceed to the next question

c. **Threat to Existing Parties**—would disposition of the action in the nonparty's absence leave existing parties subject to a substantial risk of incurring multiple or inconsistent obligations by reason of the non-party's claimed interest relating to the subject of the action?

i. **Yes.** If so, the nonparty is a necessary party. Proceed to the feasibility analysis

ii. **No.** If not, and the previous questions have received negative responses, the nonparty is not a necessary party whose joinder may be compelled under Rule 19.

2. **Feasibility of Joinder**—if a nonparty is deemed to be a necessary party, is their joinder in the action feasible?

a. **Personal Jurisdiction**—can the court obtain personal jurisdiction over the necessary party? Refer to the personal jurisdiction checklist in Chapter 1 for the necessary analysis:

   i. **No.** If not, then the joinder of the necessary party is not feasible. Proceed to Part C.3 to determine whether the party is indispensable.

   ii. **Yes.** If so, proceed to the next question.

b. **Subject Matter Jurisdiction**—will the joinder of the party deprive the court of subject matter jurisdiction over the action? Refer to the subject matter jurisdiction checklist in Chapter 3 to determine whether the court would have subject matter jurisdiction over the claim.

   i. **Yes.** If the court would be deprived of subject matter jurisdiction, the joinder of the necessary party is not feasible. Proceed to Part C.3 to determine whether the party is indispensable.

   ii. **No.** If not, proceed to the next question.

c. **Venue**—has the necessary party objected to venue?

   i. **Yes.** If so, does joinder of that party render venue improper? Refer to the venue checklist in Chapter 4 for the appropriate analysis.

   - **Yes.** If so, the necessary party must be dismissed from the action. Proceed to Part C.3 to determine whether the party is indispensable.

   - **No.** If not, and personal jurisdiction and subject matter jurisdiction exist, the joinder of the necessary party is feasible and the party must be joined in the action.

    ii. **No.** If the necessary party has not objected to venue, and personal jurisdiction and subject matter jurisdiction exist, the joinder of the party is feasible and the party must be joined in the action.

3. **Indispensability of the Party**—if joinder of the necessary party is not feasible, should the court dismiss the action in the party's absence?

  a. **Lessening of Prejudice**—can the prejudice to existing parties or the necessary party that would result from the necessary party's absence be lessened or avoided through protective provisions in the judgment, the shaping of relief, or other measures?

    i. **Yes.** If so, that suggests that the necessary party may not be considered indispensable; the court could retain jurisdiction over the case and shape relief to protect the relevant party's interests. However, this must be evaluated with reference to the next question.

    ii. **No.** If not, that would suggest the court should consider the necessary party to be indispensable. However, this must be evaluated with reference to the next question.

  b. **Adequacy of Remedy**—will the judgment rendered in the absence of the necessary party be adequate from the plaintiff's perspective?

    i. **No.** If not, that favors a determination that the necessary party is indispensable. Proceed to the next question.

    ii. **Yes.** If so, that suggests that the necessary party might not be considered indispensable, if there is no prejudice or prejudice can be lessened or avoided. If prejudice cannot be avoided, proceed to the next question.

  c. **Adequate Remedy Elsewhere**—if the action is dismissed, will the plaintiff have an adequate remedy?

    i. **Yes.** If the plaintiff can obtain adequate relief if the action is dismissed, then that would favor a determination that a party is indispensable and the action should be dismissed.

ii. **No.** If not, that suggests that the party should not be deemed to be indispensable and the action should not be dismissed.

ILLUSTRATIVE PROBLEMS

Now, here are some problems that will enable us to see how this checklist can be used to resolve joinder questions:

■ PROBLEM 7.1 ■

Enzo, a New Jersey citizen, filed a complaint against Sonny and Vito, both New Yorkers, in federal court for assault and intentional infliction of emotional distress arising out of an incident where Sonny came to collect money due to him. Enzo sought $50,000 in damages for the assault and $50,000 for the emotional distress against each defendant.

Sonny counterclaimed against Enzo for an action on his alleged debt of $40,000. Sonny also crossclaimed against Vito, alleging that if Sonny is liable to Enzo on the assault, Vito is liable to Sonny, since he was merely acting as Vito's agent when he allegedly assaulted Enzo.

Is there subject matter jurisdiction over Enzo's claims? Are Sonny's claims permissible and are either of them compulsory? Are there any jurisdictional problems with either claim?

Analysis

Jurisdiction over Enzo's Claims

Diversity jurisdiction exists over Enzo's claims. First, there is complete diversity between the parties on either side of the "v." in this action: Enzo is from New Jersey and Sonny and Vito are from New York. Regarding the amount in controversy, Enzo's claims against Vito may be aggregated, because multiple claims of a plaintiff against one defendant may be. The same analysis holds for Enzo's claims against Sonny.

Sonny's Debt Claim

To determine whether Sonny's claim against Enzo is permissible, we should first note that Sonny's claim is being made against a party who has brought a claim against him. As such, Sonny is a defending party asserting a claim against an opposing party. In that circumstance, Sonny's claim will be considered a counterclaim.

The question then becomes whether this counterclaim is compulsory. To determine whether the counterclaim is compulsory, ask whether the counterclaim arises out of the same transaction or occurrence as the claim brought against Sonny. Using the logical relationship test, it appears that Sonny's counterclaim for debt does not arise out of the same transaction or occurrence as Enzo's claim for assault because these are two separate matters the proof of which would depend on distinct bodies of evidence. Were separate trials on these claims held, no duplicative litigation would result.

Because the counterclaim does not arise out of the same transaction and occurrence, it is merely permissive and thus must independently qualify for subject matter jurisdiction to be asserted. Sonny and Enzo are diverse from one another; however, the amount in controversy for Sonny's claim is only $40,000, which is below the jurisdictional amount. Thus, no diversity jurisdiction exists. Can there be supplemental jurisdiction over the claim? Not in this instance, because the claim does not arise from a common nucleus of operative fact as Enzo's assault claim.

Sonny's Claim against Vito

To determine whether Sonny's claim against Vito is permissible, first note that Sonny's claim is being asserted against a party who has not asserted a claim against him. The question then becomes, "Against whom is Sonny's claim being asserted?" Vito is a coparty to Sonny; thus, Sonny's claim would be considered a crossclaim, and is permissible only if the claim is transactionally related to or is asserting derivative liability for Enzo's claim against Sonny. Here, Sonny is claiming that Vito is liable to him in the event that Sonny is judged to be liable to Enzo for the assault because Sonny was acting on behalf of Vito in assaulting Enzo. This is a derivative or contingent liability claim that may be brought as a crossclaim. Does the claim have to be brought? No; crossclaims are never compulsory.

Is there subject matter jurisdiction over Sonny's crossclaim? Because Sonny and Vito are not diverse, this tort claim would have to qualify for supplemental jurisdiction to be heard. Sonny's claim arises out of a common nucleus of operative fact as Enzo's assault claim because it is a claim of liability that arises directly out of Enzo's assault claim. Thus, there would be supplemental jurisdiction over Sonny's crossclaim unless Section 1367(b) of the supplemental jurisdiction statute operates to deny jurisdiction. Here, that turns out not to be the case; Sonny's crossclaim is being made by a defendant, not a plaintiff, and thus 1367(b) does not apply. Thus, Sonny's crossclaim against Vito qualifies for supplemental jurisdiction.

■ PROBLEM 7.2 ■

Same facts as above. Sonny amends his counterclaim to seek payment on an $80,000 debt: the $40,000 principal plus $40,000 in interest. In response, Enzo decides to assert a violation of the Federal Extortion Act, a law aimed at permitting victims of inter-state extortion (using threats to extract payments) to bring their actions in federal court and seek treble damages. Enzo's claim under the FEA is based on Sonny's alleged threat to harm his business if the business did not pay Sonny $40,000 a year. Enzo wants to bring the FEA claim against Sonny and Vito, since he believes that Sonny was acting as Vito's agent in seeking the payment.

Is there subject matter jurisdiction over Sonny's amended counterclaim? How should Enzo's FEA claims be treated (what type of claims are they)? May Enzo assert the FEA claims under the Rules? Must he bring either of the FEA claims?

Analysis

Subject Matter Jurisdiction over Sonny's Amended Counterclaim

This is a bit of a review question. We already know that Sonny's counterclaim is merely permissive because it is unrelated to Enzo's claim against Sonny. Thus, supplemental jurisdiction is not available. Does the amended counterclaim qualify for subject matter jurisdiction on its own? Here, Sonny is diverse from Enzo, since Sonny is from New York and Enzo is from New Jersey. Regarding the amount in controversy, Sonny may aggregate principal and interest owed on a debt to reach the jurisdictional amount. Thus, the amount in controversy requirement is now satisfied, because Sonny is seeking $80,000 when interest is taken into account. Because there is diversity of citizenship and the amount in controversy exceeds $75,000, there is diversity jurisdiction over Sonny's counterclaim.

Enzo's Claims

Because Sonny has successfully asserted a counterclaim against Enzo, Enzo is now a defending party with respect to Sonny. As such, any claims Enzo has against Sonny may be asserted as counterclaims (Enzo could also assert claims by joining them to his original claim under Rule 18(a)). The question then becomes, "*Must* Enzo assert his claim against Sonny?" That question is resolved by asking whether the claim arises out of the same transaction and occurrence as Sonny's claim against Enzo.

Enzo's FEA claim against Sonny alleges that the debt Enzo allegedly owes Sonny was incurred on the basis of threats in violation of federal law. There thus seems to be a logical relationship between the two claims, since they are both based on the same debt and proof of both claims will likely relate to the circumstances surrounding the debt and its validity. Because there is a logical relationship between the two claims, they arise out of the same transaction and occurrence; that means that Enzo's FEA claim against Sonny must be asserted as a compulsory counterclaim. What about Enzo's FEA claim against Vito? Vito has not asserted any claims against Enzo, so no counterclaims are yet permissible. Neither is Vito a coparty, which means that Enzo cannot assert the claim as a crossclaim. However, Enzo has already asserted an assault claim and an intentional infliction of emotional distress claim against Vito as a defendant. Thus, Rule 18(a) permits Enzo to join his FEA claim with those already asserted claims, even though they are not transactionally related.

Figure 7.1 provides a diagram of how the action now looks with all of these claims being asserted:

Figure 7.1 – Diagram of Claims

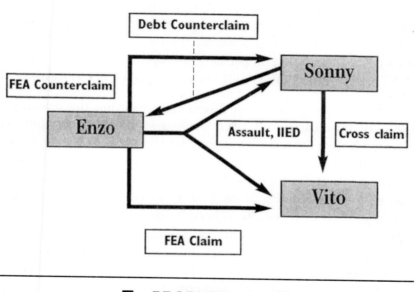

■ PROBLEM 7.3 ■

Same facts as Problem 7.1. After a trial is held Vito is found liable for $50,000 on Enzo's assault claim. Sonny is found liable for $50,000 on Enzo's emotional distress claim.

Vito, who has now moved to Nevada, files an indemnity claim in New York federal court seeking to recover $50,000 from Sonny on a derivative liability theory arising from Sonny's assault of Enzo.

Vito also brings a claim against Sonny for breach of contract for failing to contribute a promised $25,000 to Vito's new gambling venture and a separate claim for $1,000 for a plane ticket Vito bought Sonny on the promise that he would be repaid.

Does the court have subject matter jurisdiction over Vito's claims? If so, can Sonny challenge Vito's right to bring any of his claims on some other ground? If Sonny's challenge is successful, what would be the impact on Vito's remaining claims?

Analysis

Subject matter jurisdiction over Vito's claims exists on the basis of diversity jurisdiction here because he may aggregate his separate claims against a single defendant, Sonny, to reach the required jurisdictional amount and because the two parties are now diverse (Vito is now from Nevada and Sonny is a New York citizen).

Sonny should challenge Vito's right to bring the indemnity claim because it should have been asserted as a compulsory counterclaim in the earlier action involving Enzo. Once Sonny crossclaimed against Vito in the original action, Vito became a defending party with respect to Sonny and Sonny became an opposing party. As such, under Rule 13(a) Vito was then obliged to advance all transactionally related claims he had at that time against Sonny. Because his current claim for reimbursement of the amount he had to pay Enzo existed in the earlier action once Enzo asserted his claims against Vito, and the claim arises out of the same transaction and occurrence as Sonny's derivative liability cross-claim, Vito was required to raise his own derivative liability claim against Sonny. Because he failed to do so, he has waived that claim and may not raise it now.

If Sonny's challenge is successful, Vito's remaining claims will not satisfy the amount in controversy requirement for diversity jurisdiction because the $50,000 claim will be barred. Thus, the remaining claims will have to be dismissed for lack of subject matter jurisdiction.

POINTS TO REMEMBER

- Joinder is a topic where diagramming the attempted claims will really help. Before you begin your analysis, take the time to sketch out the posture of the parties and the claims being asserted by each against the other.

- Recognize the connection between joinder issues and issues of subject matter jurisdiction and venue. Whether a counterclaim, crossclaim, or a claim against a third party may be heard by the court depends on whether such claims can independently satisfy the requirements of venue and subject matter jurisdiction (and, in the case of third-party claims, personal jurisdiction). Thus, it will generally be necessary to engage in a venue or subject matter jurisdiction analysis in the context of a joinder question. Personal jurisdiction becomes a factor when new parties are being joined.

- Although there are several tests for determining whether a counterclaim arises from the same transaction or occurrence as an original claim, the predominant test is the logical relationship test. However, this test is interpreted in different ways by different courts. In applying the test in an examination context, always refer to the policy behind compulsory counterclaims—the avoidance of fragmented, duplicative litigation—to evaluate whether a counterclaim should be considered compulsory.

- Look out for coparties against whom crossclaims have been filed. They are now adversaries against the crossclaimant and must assert any available compulsory counterclaims.

*

CHAPTER 8

Discovery

]%biscovery is the process whereby parties to an action are able to obtain information from their adversaries regarding the various issues presented in the dispute. The Federal Rules of Civil Procedure as adopted in 1938 provided for very broad discovery, something that was generally not the case prior to adoption of the rules. Although several amendments to the discovery rules have restricted discovery in various ways, discovery under the Federal Rules remains remarkably broad in its scope.

Federal civil discovery is governed by Rules 26 through 37 of the Federal Rules of Civil Procedure. The content of these rules could by itself occupy an entire course or textbook. Thus, here we will focus on those aspects of these rules typically covered in the basic first-year civil procedure course: the general scope of discovery, the workings of the six discovery mechanisms, and the nature of material that is protected from disclosure.

DISCOVERY REVIEW

The Scope of Discovery

Although the scope of discoverable information has been reduced in the wake of the 2000 amendments to the federal rules, the scope of discovery in the federal system remains quite broad. Under Rule 26, parties may discover "any nonprivileged matter that is relevant to any party's claim or defense."[1] Tying the permissible scope of discovery to the claims or defenses raised by the parties gives the pleadings a significant role in determining whether given material will be discoverable. Rule 26 further provides that to be discoverable, relevant information does not have to be admissible at trial; material is discoverable so long as it appears reasonably calculated to lead to the discovery of admissible evidence.[2]

Courts have discretion to broaden or limit the scope of discovery as provided by the rules. Rule 26 provides that for "good cause" the court may permit discovery of "any matter relevant to the subject matter" of the action, the broader scope of discovery that existed prior to the 2000 amendments.[3] But the court must also limit discovery if it makes any of the following determinations provided for in Rule 26: The discovery sought is unreasonably cumulative or duplicative; the discovery sought is obtainable from some other source that is more convenient, less burdensome, or less expensive; the party seeking discovery has had ample opportunity through discovery to obtain the information sought; or the burden or expense of the proposed discovery outweighs its likely benefit, taking into account the needs of the case, the amount in controversy, the parties' resources, the importance of the issues at stake, and the importance of the proposed discovery in resolving the issues.[4] The court can limit discovery for other reasons such as to protect privacy or to prevent harassment or undue delay.

After being amended in 2006, Rule 26 now also sets forth specific limitations concerning the discovery of electronically stored information (ESI) such as emails or word processing document files. If a party indicates that a particular source of ESI is not reasonably accessible because of undue burden or cost, that party need not provide discovery of such information.[5] However, the requesting party may obtain an order compelling discovery of the information if the party from whom discovery is sought is unable to

---

1. FED. R. CIV. P. 26(b)(1).   4. FED. R. CIV. P. 26(b)(2)(C).

2. *Id.*   5. FED. R. CIV. P. 26(b)(2)(B).

3. *Id.*

show that the information is "not reasonably accessible because of undue burden or cost."[6] Even if the producing party makes such a showing, the court may still order discovery from the source if the requesting party shows good cause, but the court may also place special conditions on the discovery such as an order that the parties will share the costs associated with retrieving the information.[7] Whether discovery of not reasonably accessible ESI will be ordered and whether the costs of such discovery will be shared are determined with reference to the cost-benefit factors found in Rule 26(b)(2)(C).

Discovery Devices

The federal rules provide for six different devices parties may use to obtain information during discovery. The first are *initial disclosures*, which Rule 26(a) requires each party to make at the beginning of discovery without awaiting a discovery request. These disclosures must include information regarding the likely custodians of discoverable material, a description of documents that are likely to be used to support a party's case, a computation of damages and any documents on which such computation is based, and a copy of any insurance agreement that would be available to satisfy part or all of a judgment in the case.

Beyond these initial disclosures, the parties may seek information from parties by using one of several methods. *Depositions*, which can be oral or written, involve taking the testimony of witnesses prior to trial to obtain discoverable information through testimony. *Interrogatories* are written questions posed by one party to another in order to elicit informative responses. *Document requests* can be served on parties in order to compel the production of certain documents that pertain to topical areas of interest. Where a party's physical or mental health is at issue in a dispute, parties can use *physical and mental examinations* to obtain relevant information about a party and their claims. Finally, *requests for admission* are

---

6. *Id.*

7. *Id. See* Zubulake v. UBS Warburg LLC, 216 F.R.D. 18, 20 (S.D.N.Y. 2003) (ordering the plaintiff to pay twenty-five percent of the costs associated with restoring UBS backup tapes for purposes of discovery).

statements served on another party with the request that the statements be specifically admitted or denied; any admissions garnered from this process will be conclusive evidence at trial with regard to those matters admitted.

If a party refuses to comply with the discovery request of another, the requesting party must confer with the disclosing party to try to reach some type of agreement regarding the discovery request. If no resolution can be achieved during the conference, the disgruntled party may approach the court seeking an order resolving the dispute in its favor. If the disgruntled party is the party seeking the information, that party can seek a *motion to compel* from the court, which if granted would order the resisting party to disclose the information, over its objection. If the disgruntled party is the disclosing party, that party can seek a *protective order*, whereby the court orders that the information is protected from discovery and need not be disclosed, or orders that the material will be disclosed but in a limited or somehow protected way that addresses the disclosing party's concerns. For example, if a party is concerned about confidential membership information being revealed to others, the court can order that the information not be revealed to non-parties or that the material be redacted so that sensitive information remains confidential.[8]

Once material is disclosed pursuant to discovery obligations, all parties have a continuing obligation to supplement their production if the information becomes incomplete due to new information or if the disclosed information is discovered to be incorrect in some respect. The failure to comply with this or any other discovery obligation can result in sanctions under Rule 26(g). That rule provides that attorneys signing discovery documents certify that all disclosures are complete and correct and that all discovery requests are warranted under the law, are not meant to harass or cause unnecessary delay or expense, and are not unreasonably burdensome. Violations are punishable by sanctions including paying the adversaries' costs arising out of the violation.

---

8. Marrese v. Am. Acad. of Ortho. Surgeons, 726 F.2d 1150 (7th Cir. 1985).

Privileged Materials

Certain material is protected from discovery notwithstanding its relevance to one of the claims or defenses made by a party to the action. Rule 26(b)(1) provides for the discovery of any "nonprivileged" matter that is relevant to a claim or defense in the action. Matter can be privileged based on one of any number of evidentiary privileges recognized by the applicable substantive law where the case is being heard. Such privileges include the privileges for communications between attorney and client, doctor and patient, husband and wife, and priest and penitent.

If information is protected by a privilege, it does not have to be disclosed at all. The policy behind extending a privilege to certain communications is the promotion of free communication in the context of these important social and legal relationships; free communication in these contexts is deemed to be a superior societal interest than the ability to have such information available as evidence in litigation.

Although privilege protects certain confidential communications, the Supreme Court has made it clear that the underlying facts embodied in such communications are not entitled to protection.[9] The reason for this rule is clear; if facts could be protected by disclosing them to one's attorney it would be too easy to immunize all relevant information from compelled disclosure to others.

Privileged communications lose their protection if they are disclosed to third parties that are not part of the confidential relationship. Once such waiver occurs, a party can be forced to disclose all communications involving the same subject matter. The purpose of this rule is to prevent selective waiver for the benefit of the privilege holder. If one could waive the privilege with respect to certain communications because doing so was beneficial to their case, but then refuse access to related communications that were

---

9. Upjohn Co. v. United States, 449 U.S. 383, 395 (1981) ("The privilege only protects from disclosure of communications; it does not protect disclosure of the underlying facts by those who communicate with the attorney.").

harmful citing privilege, a party could unfairly use the privilege both as a shield and a sword.

There are four general requirements that must be satisfied in order to establish the attorney-client privilege. First, there must be a communication; private memos or notes that are not communicated to others will not qualify for protection. Next, the communication must be kept in confidence, meaning that only the parties to the confidential relationship are privy to the conversation or communication when it occurs. Third, the communication must be between an attorney acting in the capacity of an attorney and that attorney's client, a requirement that prevents those who happen to be attorneys working in other capacities from being able to invoke the privilege by their mere involvement in a communication. Finally, the communication must be engaged in for the purposes of soliciting or providing legal advice. If all of these requirements are met, the privilege may be asserted, unless it has been waived or confidentiality has somehow been breached.

In the corporate context, the Supreme Court has ruled that privilege applies with the same force as it does in non-corporate situations. For corporations, the test of whether the privilege will attach is whether the communication at issue is between counsel for the corporation acting as legal counsel, and any corporate employee in order to solicit or receive legal advice.[10] This standard would also treat communications between non-attorney employees as privileged where their communications are at the behest of counsel for the purpose of distributing or formulating legal advice.

Work-Product Doctrine

There is another category of information that is protected from discovery: so-called trial preparation materials or work product. Work product refers to any material prepared in anticipation of litigation or for trial by or for another party or by or for that other party's representative.[11] Although now largely protected by rule, protection for work product was originally developed by the

---

10. *Id.*   **11.** FED. R. CIV. P. 26(b)(3).

Supreme Court in ***Hickman v. Taylor***.[12] In *Hickman*, the Court indicated that material prepared in anticipation of litigation was not discoverable absent a showing of substantial need and the inability to obtain the information elsewhere. The Court went on to indicate that under no circumstances were the mental impressions, thoughts, or legal opinions of legal counsel discoverable, regardless of whatever showing a party could make.

Rule 26(b)(3) codified most of *Hickman* by making these standards an express part of the Federal Rules. However, Rule 26(b)(3) limits its protection to "documents and tangible things" a limit *Hickman* did not impose. *Hickman*'s view of the work-product doctrine protects intangible materials and thus that case can be relied upon where Rule 26(b)(3) falls short.

DISCOVERY CHECKLIST

With that backdrop, here is the checklist for analyzing problems presenting questions in the discovery area:

A. **DISCOVERABILITY**—is the material requested discoverable under the Federal Rules?

   1. **Relevance**—is the material relevant to a claim or defense of any party in the action?

       a. **No.** If the claim is not relevant to a claim or defense, it is beyond the permissible scope of discovery absent an order from the court permitting discovery of material relevant to the subject matter of the action.

       b. **Yes.** If the material is relevant to a claim or defense, it is discoverable, unless the court decides to limit the discovery or it is material that is protected from discovery.

   2. **Limitations**—do circumstances exist that require the court to limit discovery of the material in question? The court is

---

12.   329 U.S. 495 (1947).

required to limit discovery if any of the following questions can be answered in the affirmative:

a. **Duplicative**—is the requested material unreasonably cumulative or duplicative of material already sought and received?

b. **Less Burdensome Alternative**—is the requested material obtainable from some other source that is more convenient, less burdensome, or less expensive?

c. **Missed Opportunity**—has the requesting party had ample opportunity by discovery to obtain the information sought?

d. **Cost Surpasses Benefit**—does the burden or expense of the proposed discovery outweigh its likely benefit? This question applies particularly to electronically stored information, which need not be produced if it is contained within sources that are not reasonably accessible because of undue burden or cost. The following factors are to be considered when determining whether burdensome, costly, or not reasonably accessible information should be produced:

    i. The needs of the case;

    ii. The amount in controversy;

    iii. The parties' resources;

    iv. The importance of the issues at stake in the litigation; and

    v. The importance of the proposed discovery in resolving the issues.

3. **Protective Orders**—are there circumstances that would permit the court to limit the discoverability of the material through entry of a protective order? That question is answered with reference to the following question: Is there a need to protect a party or person from annoyance, embarrassment, oppression, or undue burden or expense?

a. **Yes.** If so, the court may enter a protective order that orders any one of the following:

    i. The discovery will not be had;

ii. The discovery may be had only on specified terms and conditions;

iii. The discovery may be had only by a method of discovery other than that selected by the party seeking discovery;

iv. That certain matters not be inquired into or that the discovery be limited to certain matters;

v. That the discovery be conducted with no one present except persons designated by the court;

vi. That a deposition after being sealed be opened only by order of the court;

vii. That a trade secret or other confidential information not be revealed or only be revealed in a designated way; or

viii. That the parties simultaneously file specified documents or information enclosed in sealed envelopes as directed by the court.

b. **No.** If there is no need for protection, the court will not enter a protective order covering the requested material.

B. **ATTORNEY-CLIENT PRIVILEGE**—assuming the material is discoverable and there are no limitations or protective orders imposed on discovery of the material in question, is the material privileged from disclosure?

1. **Communication**—does the material pertain to a communication?

   a. **No.** If not, the information is not protected by the attorney-client privilege and will be discoverable unless work-product protection applies.

   b. **Yes.** If so, proceed to the next question.

2. **Confidentiality**—did the communication occur in confidence exclusive of any third parties not party to the privileged relationship?

   a. **No.** If not, the information is not protected by the attorney-client privilege and will be discoverable unless work-product protection applies.

b. **Yes.** If so, proceed to the next question.

3. **Between an Attorney and Client**—did the communication involve an attorney acting as such and their client or was the communication among the client's employees generated by or at the behest of an attorney acting as such?

   a. **No.** If not, the information is not protected by the attorney-client privilege and will be discoverable unless work-product protection applies.

   b. **Yes.** If so, proceed to the next question.

4. **Legal Advice**—was the communication for the purpose of giving or seeking legal advice?

   a. **No.** If not, the information is not protected by the attorney-client privilege and will be discoverable unless work-product protection applies.

   b. **Yes.** If so, proceed to the next question.

5. **Waiver**—if the answer to each of the above questions is *yes*, was the privilege waived by disclosure of the communication to third parties outside of the privileged relationship?

   a. **No.** If not, the privilege applies to the material and it is not discoverable and need not be disclosed.

   b. **Yes.** If so, the privilege has been waived and may not be asserted to prevent disclosure of the material. However, proceed to Part C to determine whether work-product protection applies.

C. **WORK-PRODUCT PROTECTION**—is the material protected from discovery by the work-product doctrine?

   1. **Legal Thoughts**—does the material contain the mental impressions, conclusions, opinions, or legal theories of an attorney or other representative of the party concerning the litigation?

      a. **Yes.** If so, that portion of the material may not be disclosed under any circumstances. Proceed to the next question to determine whether any remaining material must be disclosed.

    b. **No.** If not, proceed to the next question to see if the material is protected work product.

2. **Trial Preparation**—were the materials prepared in anticipation of litigation?

    a. **Yes.** If so, proceed to the next question.

    b. **No.** If not, the material is not protected by the work-product doctrine.

3. **Preparer of Material**—was the material prepared by or for the party receiving the request or by or for that party's representative?

    a. **Yes.** If so, the material is protected work product. Proceed to the next question to determine whether the court can nonetheless order it to be disclosed to the requesting party.

    b. **No.** If not, then the party receiving the request may not claim work-product protection over the material and will have to disclose it.

4. **Substantial Need**—can the party requesting the material demonstrate they have a substantial need for the materials to prepare their case?

    a. **No.** If not, the party will not be able to overcome the objection that the material is protected work product.

    b. **Yes.** If so, proceed to the next question.

5. **Other Means**—can the party requesting the material demonstrate that it is unable, without undue hardship, to obtain the substantial equivalent of the materials by some other means?

    a. **Yes.** If so, the court may order that the work product be disclosed to the requesting party.

    b. **No.** If not, the party will not be able to overcome the objection that the material is protected work product.

ILLUSTRATIVE PROBLEM

Now, here is a problem that will enable us to see how this checklist can be used to resolve discovery questions:

■ PROBLEM 8.1 ■

Xenon Corp. sues Petroleos de Peru (PDP) for breach of their crude oil supply agreement, alleging that PDP failed to supply crude to Xenon at agreed upon discounted prices. During discovery, Xenon files a document request seeking all documents relating to the sale of crude to all of PDP's customers, all documents revealing or discussing pricing for such sales, and all minutes of PDP's Board meetings from the past 20 years.

PDP's counsel objects to the production of the Board minutes on the ground that these documents are beyond the permissible scope of discovery and on the ground that they contain commercially sensitive information. PDP's counsel also withholds all documents discussing pricing for the sale of crude because in each and every discussion involving the setting of crude prices, an attorney from PDP's general counsel's office was involved in order to make sure that prices comported with PDP's contractual obligations under the various crude oil supply agreements PDP had with its respective customers.

When Xenon confers with PDP in an effort to resolve this dispute, PDP explains that in-house counsel was always an integral part of every pricing discussion and decision in order to provide legal advice regarding the propriety of the prices and thus the material is privileged. PDP also explains that it will not produce all Board minutes because these include material that is not relevant to Xenon's claims and are highly sensitive.

After conferring with PDP, Xenon notices that on PDP's privilege log employees from NG, Inc.—a separate company with whom PDP often engages in joint ventures—are listed as additional recipients of each of these pricing discussion memoranda and emails. Feeling that it has a right to both the pricing discussion documents and all of the board minutes, Xenon moves for an order to compel from the court. How should the court rule?

Analysis

At issue here is whether PDP must produce its pricing documents and board minutes. The pricing documents are clearly relevant to the claim in the case that PDP did not adhere to an agreement regarding pricing it would offer to Xenon versus other customers.

Xenon's objection to the production of these documents is not on relevance grounds but rather on the ground that they are protected by the attorney-client privilege. To receive the protection of the privilege, the documents would have to reveal communications between attorneys and clients, in confidence, regarding the solicitation or delivery of legal advice. Here, although attorneys may have been involved in the communications embodied in these documents, the facts reveal that third parties not party to the attorney-client relationship (NG employees) were also privy to these documents. Thus, the key requirement of confidentiality is not present here and the documents cannot be protected by the privilege. The court should thus order PDP to produce the pricing documents.

Regarding the Board minutes, certainly not all of the Board's minutes will be relevant to the claim raised by Xenon. Only those minutes revealing pricing discussions and possibly those discussing sales to other customers in general would be likely to lead to the discovery of admissible evidence. The court should thus order the production of only those minutes that are relevant to Xenon's claim. As for the commercial sensitivity of the minutes, their sensitivity will not prevent relevant information from being discovered; rather, the court can issue a protective order that ensures that only key people at Xenon see the information and that it is not disclosed beyond those individuals.

POINTS TO REMEMBER

- Discoverable material need not be admissible at trial. So long as the material is likely to lead to admissible evidence, it is discoverable.
- The scope of discoverable material extends to all nonprivileged material relevant to a claim or defense raised in the action. This

is narrower than the pre-2000 standard of relevance to the subject matter of the action; however, the court can expand the scope of discovery to that standard upon request.

- When the discovery of electronically stored information is at issue, a party is not required to produce such information from sources that it deems to be not reasonably accessible. Under such circumstances, the opposing party may seek to compel such discovery for good cause, but may be required to share some of the costs of producing the information.

- Be on the lookout for waiver or lack of confidentiality for privilege questions. The presence of or disclosure to any third parties who are not part of the privileged relationship will destroy the privilege.

- Work product is a broader doctrine than the attorney-client privilege in that the material need not have been prepared by counsel to be protected. However, work-product doctrine is weaker than the privilege in that it can be overcome if a sufficient showing is made.

CHAPTER 9

Pre-Answer Motions & Summary Judgment

The Federal Rules provide for preliminary disposition of cases without trial through several procedural mechanisms. The devices typically covered in the basic first-year civil procedure course are those housed within Rule 12—often referred to as pre-answer motions—and the motion for summary judgment, which is governed by Rule 56. This chapter will focus on the standards and analyses applicable to these motions.

REVIEW OF PRE–ANSWER MOTIONS

Federal Rule 12 provides several defenses and objections a party can raise prior to the filing of an answer, within the body of an answer, or at some time after the closing of the pleadings. These defenses include lack of subject matter jurisdiction, lack of personal jurisdiction, improper venue, insufficiency of process, insufficiency of service of process, failure to state a claim upon which relief can be granted, and failure to join a party under Rule 19.[1] Each of these defenses may be raised by motion. Rule 12 also provides for a separate motion, a motion for judgment on the pleadings, as a means of preliminarily dismissing an action.[2]

---

1. Fed. R. Civ. P. 12(b).   2. Fed. R. Civ. P. 12(c).

Whether a court will grant motions to dismiss for lack of subject matter jurisdiction, lack of personal jurisdiction, improper venue, insufficiency of process, insufficiency of service of process, and failure to join a party under Rule 19 depends on the rules and principles that govern each of those respective areas. Thus, to determine whether a motion to dismiss for lack of personal jurisdiction should be granted, one has to refer to the law of personal jurisdiction and engage in an analysis of the facts based on legal precedent in that area. The same holds true for motions to dismiss on each of these other grounds; this book has already provided the reader with checklists that aid in each of these analyses, except for insufficiency of process and service of process. A motion challenging process or service of process is simply evaluated with reference to the requirements set forth in Rule 4.

The motion to dismiss for failure to state a claim and the motion for judgment on the pleadings require further explication. These motions do not refer to the procedural issues of jurisdiction, process, and joinder but rather address the substantive legal sufficiency of the claims asserted by a party in its complaint (or the counterclaims in a party's answer). Specifically, the motion to dismiss for failure to state a claim, which is provided for by Rule 12(b)(6), asserts that even if the allegations in the complaint are taken to be true, no legal claim is stated and the complaint should thus be dismissed. A motion for judgment on the pleadings (Rule 12(c)) makes the same assertion, but simply does so on the basis of a complete set of pleadings. In both motions, the challenging party is asserting that the law does not recognize the facts that have been pleaded as stating an actionable claim for which a remedy is available. When such is the case, there would be little point in moving forward with the case because no legal claim properly exists.

To evaluate a motion to dismiss for failure to state a claim,[3] the court is required to assume the truth of all of the allegations

---

3. Because the standard for a motion for judgment on the pleadings is identical to that of a motion to dismiss for failure to state a claim, *see* Patel v. Contemporary Classics of Beverly Hills, 259 F.3d 123, 126 (2d Cir. 2001), the discussion herein will simply discuss the relevant standards with reference to the 12(b)(6) motion to dismiss without men-

contained within the party's complaint. Further, the court must construe the complaint in the light most favorable to the plaintiff with all doubts resolved in his favor. If it may be reasonably anticipated that the plaintiff, on the basis of what has been alleged, could make out a case at trial entitling her to some relief, the complaint should not be dismissed. This means that even if it is possible to read a complaint as not stating a claim, if a plausible reading does state a claim, the complaint cannot be dismissed. However, keep in mind that after the Supreme Court's decision in **Bell Atlantic Corp. v. Twombly** a court may dismiss a complaint that includes mere legal conclusions rather than facts showing plausible entitlement to relief.[4]

Because the purpose of a motion to dismiss for failure to state a claim is to challenge the legal sufficiency of a complaint, a motion that calls facts into question will not prevail under a Rule 12(b)(6). However, if the motion is accompanied by additional supporting factual material beyond the pleadings, the motion will be converted into a summary judgment motion and considered under the standards of Rule 56. Where the complaint itself reveals facts that, if true, would conclusively bar recovery, a 12(b)(6) motion will prevail.[5] Additionally, a complaint does not fail to state a claim merely because it does not set forth a complete and convincing picture of the alleged wrongdoing. Finally, if the complaint contains both valid and invalid claims, only the invalid claims—not the complaint as a whole—will be dismissed.

Beyond understanding the substantive standard for granting the various motions under Rule 12, it is important to have an understanding of when and how each of these motions may be raised under the rules. Of the motions provided for in Rule 12(b), four are required to be made initially, in a responding party's first

---

tioning the motion for judgment on the pleadings.

4. 127 S. Ct. 1955, 1964–65 (2007) ("[A] plaintiff's obligation to provide the grounds of his entitlement to relief requires more than labels and conclusions, and a formulaic

recitation of the elements of a cause of action will not do.").

5. *See, e.g.,* Am. Nurses' Ass'n v. Illinois (7th Cir. 1986).

response to the complaint, or they will be deemed waived. Specifically, the motions to dismiss for lack of personal jurisdiction, improper venue, insufficient process, and insufficient service of process must each be raised by pre-answer motion or, in the absence of such a motion, in the defending party's first responsive pleading.[6] Further, these motions, when made, must be consolidated and made together if they are to be made at all[7]; this rule prevents piecemeal and dilatory attacks on complaints by the filing of successive motions under the rule.

The remaining Rule 12 objections and defenses need not be raised initially. The defenses of failure to state a claim upon which relief can be granted and failure to join an indispensable party under Rule 19 can be raised in any of the pleadings, by motion for judgment on the pleadings, or at trial.[8] The defense of lack of subject matter jurisdiction can be raised for the first time at any time throughout the proceedings, including on appeal.[9]

So the key here is to remember those defenses that must be raised initially. Any challenges to personal jurisdiction, venue, process, or service of process must be asserted simultaneously and initially or they are waived.

SUMMARY JUDGMENT REVIEW

A separate motion that can dispose of a case preliminarily is the summary judgment motion. Provided for in Rule 56, summary judgment is a judgment entered by the court before trial on the motion of either party arguing that there is no factual dispute regarding the matter for which summary judgment is sought and thus a continuation of the action is not warranted. Motions for summary judgment go beyond the pleadings and are based on whatever factual evidence has been adduced through discovery at the time the motion is presented.

---

6. Fed. R. Civ. P. 12 (h). The rule also permits these defenses to be raised in an amendment permitted by Rule 15(a) made as a matter of course.

7. Fed. R. Civ. P. 12(g).

8. Fed. R. Civ. P. 12(h)(2).

9. Fed. R. Civ. P. 12(h)(3).

The question presented when a summary judgment motion is made is whether there is a "genuine issue as to any material fact and that the movant is entitled to judgment as a matter of law."[10] A "genuine issue" means that the factual dispute must be based on conflicting factual evidence, not simply opposing opinions or unsupported assertions or denials. A "material fact" refers to a fact that is essential to establishing an element of a claim. For example, the essential elements of negligence are duty, breach, harm, and causation. Facts pertaining to any of these elements would be considered material. When a genuine issue of material fact exists, a reasonable jury could reach different conclusions concerning the facts and thus there is reason to move forward with a trial in the case. In that event, summary judgment should be denied.

The critical issues when analyzing summary judgment problems are who bears the burdens of production and proof in the context of summary judgment motions and what each party must do to discharge their respective burdens. In *Celotex Corp. v. Catrett* the Supreme Court indicated that although parties seeking summary judgment bear an initial burden of production in the sense that they have to make a showing to the court that there is no genuine factual dispute in the case, where the nonmovant would bear the burden of proof at trial, that party also bears the burden of offering proof to support their claims in the face of a summary judgment motion.[11] The moving party in such a case can discharge its initial burden of production by producing affidavits or other evidence in support of its motion but it need not do so; the Court held in *Celotex* that movants may simply refer to the evidentiary record before the court and point out that it fails to support the nonmovant's claim.[12] In response, the party opposing the motion must "set out specific facts showing a genuine issue for trial."[13]

In *Anderson v. Liberty Lobby, Inc.* the Supreme Court added that in ruling on a motion for summary judgment the judge must be guided by the substantive evidentiary standard the jury will have

---

10. FED. R. CIV. P. 56(c).

11. 477 U.S. 317, 323–24 (1986).

12. *Id.*

13. FED. R. CIV. P. 56(e)(2).

to use at trial.[14] This requirement derives from the fact that the summary judgment motion, in the Court's view, is most appropriately viewed as an early motion for directed verdict.[15] Requiring consideration of the facts based on the evidentiary burden means that the party bearing the burden of proof in a summary judgment context will have to present evidence of a sufficient quantum to satisfy the evidentiary burden they would carry at trial, whether that be preponderance of the evidence or a clear and convincing evidence standard. Prior to *Anderson* it at least appeared that a party bearing the burden of proof for summary judgment purposes only had to present sufficient evidence to make a prima facie case.[16]

Matsushita Electrical Industrial Co. v. Zenith Radio Corp., decided by the Supreme Court the same year as *Celotex* and *Anderson*,[17] added to the burden of plaintiffs resisting summary judgment motions by allowing courts to disregard supporting evidence where it is unconvincing or fails to rule out alternate lawful explanations for the challenged conduct.[18] Although it is possible that the holding in *Matsushita* was merely a product of its antitrust context,[19] the case nevertheless presents a Court willing to countenance (and engage in) consideration of the persuasiveness of proffered evidence when making a summary judgment determination. Along with *Anderson* and *Celotex*, *Matsushita* makes it more difficult for plaintiffs resisting summary judgment motions to prevail and get to trial. Also, the entire trilogy of cases has resulted in summary judgment motions moving away from being a means of

---

14. 477 U.S. 242 (1986).

15. *Id.* at 251, 254.

16. *See id.* at 268 (Brennan, J. dissenting) (indicating that the Court's summary judgment precedents did not make "any suggestion that once a nonmoving plaintiff has made out a prima facie case based on evidence satisfying Rule 56(e) that there is any showing that a defendant can make to prevail on a motion for summary judgment"); *see also* Dolgow v. Anderson, 438 F.2d 825, 830 (2d Cir. 1970) (requiring a denial of summary judgment where the "slightest doubt" existed regarding whether the party opposing the motion might persuade a jury of the merits of its case).

17. Together, these three cases are sometimes referred to as the *Celotex* trilogy.

18. 475 U.S. 574 (1986).

19. *See* Arthur Miller, *The Pretrial Rush to Judgment: Are the "Litigation Explosion," "Liability Crisis," and Efficiency Clichés Eroding Our Day in Court and Jury Trial Commitments?*, 78 N.Y.U. L. Rev. 982, 1030 (2003).

ensuring that there would be a genuine factual dispute for the jury to resolve toward being a full "dress-rehearsal" of the trial, with the defendant having to prove relatively little and the evidentiary weighing being done by the judge rather than a jury.[20]

PRE-ANSWER MOTIONS & SUMMARY JUDGMENT CHECKLIST

With that review in mind, here is the checklist for analyzing problems presenting questions regarding pre-answer motions and summary judgment:

A. ABILITY TO RAISE THE DEFENSE—can the defense being asserted be raised at this time?

    1. Nature of Defense—is the defense claiming lack of personal jurisdiction, improper venue, ineffective process, or ineffective service of process (the waivable defenses)?

        a. **Yes.** If so, proceed to the next question.

        b. **No.** If not, the defenses or objections can be raised at any time through trial. The objection that there is a lack of subject matter jurisdiction can be raised at any time.

    2. Timing of Motion—if one of the waivable defenses is being raised, has any other defense, objection, or responsive pleading already been submitted to the court?

        a. **Yes.** If so, the waivable defense has been waived and may not be asserted.

        b. **No.** If not, the defense may be raised and must be raised along with other waivable defenses a party intends to assert.

---

20. Samuel Issacharoff & George Loewenstein, *Second Thoughts About Summary Judgment*, 100 YALE L.J. 73, 87 (1990). *See also* Linda S. Mullenix, *Summary Judgment: Taming the Beast of Burdens*, 10 AM. J. TRIAL ADVOC. 433, 468 (1987) ("By reading backwards from the directed verdict the Court transformed summary procedure into a full trial-before-trial.").

B. **VALIDITY OF THE DEFENSE (FAILURE TO STATE A CLAIM)**[21]—should the motion to dismiss for failure to state a claim be granted?

    1. **Factual Challenge?** Does the motion challenge the factual allegations of the complaint?

        a. **Yes.** If so, the motion is not properly a motion to dismiss for failure to state a claim and may not be granted. However, if such motion is supported by affidavits or other factual evidence, the motion will be converted to a summary judgment motion.

        b. **No.** If not, proceed to the next question.

    2. **Legal Challenges**—if the motion challenges the legal sufficiency of the complaint, does the complaint, assuming the allegations to be true, contain factual allegations that suggest the claimant is entitled to relief under the applicable substantive law?

        a. **Yes.** If so, the complaint properly states a legal claim and may not be dismissed under Rule 12(b) (6).

        b. **No.** If not, the complaint fails to state a claim and should be dismissed.

C. **SUMMARY JUDGMENT**—should the court enter summary judgment against a party?

    1. **Movant's Party Status**—is the movant the party bearing the burden of proof on the claim at trial?

        a. **Yes.** If so, the movant must present the court with sufficient factual evidence (from the existing record or through additional submissions) to support its claim. Proceed to the next question.

        b. **No.** If not, the movant only has the burden of showing the court that no genuine issue of material fact exists.

---

21. Remember, the validity of the other defenses can be assessed with reference to material covered in prior chapters on personal jurisdiction, subject matter jurisdiction, and venue. A motion challenging process or service of process is simply evaluated with reference to the requirements set forth in Rule 4. A motion for judgment on the pleadings will be evaluated according to the same standards indicated here for the motion to dismiss for failure to state a claim.

i.   This burden may be discharged through the presentation of affidavits or other factual evidence or simply by pointing to the existing evidence and arguing that it fails to support the nonmovants claim.

    ii. Once this is done, the nonmovant has the burden of persuasion; proceed to the next question.

2. **Discharging the Plaintiff's Burden of Proof**—has the party bearing the burden of proof at trial pointed to or presented sufficient factual evidence to support its claim such that summary judgment should not be entered?

   a.   **Admissible Evidence**—has the party carrying the burden of proof supported its claim with admissible factual evidence?

      i.   **No.** If not, the party has failed to meet its burden and summary judgment should be granted.

      ii. **Yes.** If so, proceed to the next question.

   b.   **Persuasive Evidence**—is the party's evidence persuasive or does the party's evidence disprove alternate reasonable explanations regarding the defendant's challenged conduct? ***Matsushita v. Zenith***, 475 U.S. 574 (1986).

      i.   **No.** If the party's evidence is unpersuasive, can be discounted, or fails to disprove more reasonable alternate explanations, a court *may* determine that the evidence is insufficient to create a genuine issue of material fact and enter summary judgment.

      ii. **Yes.** If the party's evidence is persuasive, proceed to the next question.

   c.   **Evidentiary Standard**—does the party's evidence prove its case to the degree required under the relevant evidentiary standard that would be applicable at trial? ***Anderson v. Liberty Lobby, Inc.***, 477 U.S. 242 (1986).

      i.   **No.** If not, summary judgment should be entered against the party.

      ii. **Yes.** If so, summary judgment should not be entered against the party.

ILLUSTRATIVE PROBLEMS

Now, here are some problems that will enable us to see how this checklist can be used to resolve questions about dismissals for failure to state a claim and summary judgment:

■ PROBLEM 9.1 ■

Ashley files the following complaint against Jessica: "The court has jurisdiction on the basis of diversity. On Jan. 1, 2002 the plaintiff gave the defendant $100,000. The defendant has not returned the $100,000 to the plaintiff. Wherefore the plaintiff demands judgment for $100,000." Upon receiving the complaint Jessica moves to dismiss the complaint for failure to state a claim under Rule 12(b)(6). How should the court rule? How could Ashley amend her complaint to fix it?

Analysis

To determine whether Ashley's complaint states a claim, the court is to ask whether the complaint, if taken to be true, would entitle Ashley to relief. Here, the complaint indicates that Ashley gave $100,000 to Jessica and that Jessica did not return the money. However, the complaint provides no indication or allegation that Jessica was under any obligation to return the money to Ashley. Ashley could have given the money to Jessica as repayment of a debt. Or, the money could have been given to Jessica as a gift. The point is that even if the court accepts that Ashley gave and Jessica failed to return $100,000, that fact alone would not entitle Ashley to the legal relief she seeks. Rather, Ashley would need to allege that she gave the money to Jessica as a loan and Jessica owed her the money as a debt (or that Jessica was simply holding the money for her temporarily and was supposed to give it back). Unless Ashley amends her complaint to make these or similar allegations, the complaint, as it currently exists, fails to state a claim that entitles her to any relief.

■ PROBLEM 9.2 ■

Stein sued Pharma Corp. for an illness allegedly resulting from his exposure to pesticides produced by Pharma. Stein alleged that he worked on a farm where Pharma's pesticides were used for over 20 years and has developed symptoms that are consistent with those that can result from harmful exposure to such chemicals. To support his case, Stein had provided the testimony of Dr. Duncan as an expert witness, who agreed in his report that Stein's symptoms were "consistent with symptoms arising in patients who have been exposed to pesticides of the variety produced and used by Pharma and to which Stein was exposed."

At the end of discovery, Pharma moved for summary judgment, claiming that although Stein had supported his claims that he was exposed to Pharma's pesticides and exhibited the relevant symptoms of harmful exposure, the evidence Stein had produced did not conclusively support his claim that pesticide exposure caused his illness because there could be many other explanations for Stein's symptoms.

In response, Stein submitted the affidavit of Dr. Duncan reaffirming the conclusions contained within his report, that Stein's symptoms are consistent with those of individuals who develop an illness in response to pesticide exposure.

How should the court rule on the motion?

Analysis

Under Rule 56, the court is to grant a motion for summary judgment when there appears to be no genuine issue of material fact and the moving party is entitled to judgment as a matter of law. The party moving for summary judgment has the initial burden of presenting to the court information sufficient to indicate the absence of a genuine issue; however, as the Court in *Celotex* indicated, where the movant does not carry the burden of proof on the matter at trial, that party may simply point to the existing record of pleadings, interrogatories, deposition records, etc., and indicate that those materials fail to support the nonmovant's case. Here, the movant is the defendant and thus does not bear the burden of proof on the claim at trial. Thus, by simply arguing that the evidence in the record fails to support Stein's claim of causation, Pharma has discharged its burden under *Celotex*.

Having satisfied its burden, the burden of proof now rests on Stein. Under *Celotex*, Stein must produce specific factual evidence that establishes the essential elements of his claim—including causation—to defeat Pharma's motion. Here, Stein has presented the affidavit of Dr. Duncan, a medical expert who is testifying that Stein's symptoms are consistent with the illness that results from pesticide exposure. Per *Anderson*, Stein's proffered evidence must be sufficient to permit a jury to find, by a preponderance of the evidence, that exposure to Pharma's pesticides caused his illness. Additionally, per *Matsushita*, Stein's evidence must disprove alternate reasonable explanations regarding the cause of his illness.

In this case, Stein's evidence does not appear to meet that burden. Although the expert affidavit submitted indicates that Stein's symptoms are consistent with pesticide exposure-induced illness, Stein's evidence neither makes it more likely than not that his illness was caused by exposure to pesticide nor does it rule out other plausible explanations for Stein's injuries. The jury would not be permitted to make a finding of liability solely on the basis of an expert report indicating that Stein's symptoms are merely "consistent" with pesticide exposure when such information does not provide evidence of causation. Thus, under the standards articulated by the Court in the *Celotex* trilogy of cases, the court should grant Pharma's motion for summary judgment.

POINTS TO REMEMBER

- Always be alert for waiver when it comes to the defenses of lack of personal jurisdiction, improper venue, insufficient process, and insufficient service of process. These defenses must be raised initially together or they are waived.

- The motion to dismiss for failure to state a claim basically says to the plaintiff, "So what? Even if what you say is true, the law does not give you any right to relief." Thus, no factual disputes are appropriately resolved here; only challenges based on legal insufficiency may be asserted via a motion to dismiss under Rule 12(b)(6).

- After *Bell Atlantic v. Twombly*, many courts are requiring complaints to include facts that substantiate generalized legal allegations. Complaints lacking such factual support may be subject to dismissal under this standard.

- The standards surrounding summary judgment are a matter of debate, controversy, and confusion. The *Celotex* trilogy unquestionably altered summary judgment standards but failed to provide the clearest of guidance regarding how to make summary judgment determinations. It might be useful to articulate these issues in the context of your own analysis on an examination.

- Remember that the movant always has the burden of showing the basis for its motion, which means that that party must demonstrate to the court how the existing record reveals an absence of a genuine issue of material fact. If the movant does not have the burden of proof at trial, however, simply pointing to the record, without producing any additional factual evidence, will suffice to shift the burden of proof to the nonmovant.

- To determine the propriety of summary judgment, ask whether a jury looking at the presented evidence would reasonably be able to reach a verdict for either side in the dispute. When one side lacks sufficient evidentiary support to permit a jury finding in its favor, a trial would be useless and summary judgment should be entered against that party.

- If the party bearing the burden of proof at trial identifies admissible factual evidence that supports its claim, as opposed to mere opinions or unsupported allegations, then summary judgment against that party should probably be denied. However, the *Anderson* and *Matsushita* holdings will complicate such a conclusion and should be considered and discussed in any exam answer.

CHAPTER 10

Judgment as a Matter of Law and the Motion for a New Trial

O nce the parties reach trial, there remain several ways that the jury can be denied the opportunity to decide the case or that their verdict can be ignored. The federal rules provide for a judgment as a matter of law—which has the court rather than the jury entering a verdict in a case—and a motion for a new trial—which gives the case to another jury for another trial. Both of these procedural devices will be reviewed in this chapter.

REVIEW OF JUDGMENT AS A MATTER OF LAW

The motion for judgment as a matter of law as provided for in Rule 50 of the Federal Rules of Civil Procedure is the federal equivalent of the traditional directed verdict motion and motion for judgment notwithstanding the verdict or j.n.o.v.[1] The principal purpose and effect of the motion for judgment as a matter of law is to take the case from the jury for resolution by the court. This is done only when the evidence presented by a party on an issue is legally

---

1. The initials "j.n.o.v." stand for judgment *non obstante veredicto.*

insufficient to support a reasonable juror's finding in favor of that party on that issue.[2]

A motion for judgment as a matter of law can be made at any time after the movant's adversary has completed the presentation of its case and before the case is submitted to the jury.[3] Because the motion is made prior to the jury's issuance of a verdict, the motion mirrors the directed verdict motion and seeks to prevent the case from being submitted to the jury at all.

The rules do provide for consideration of a motion for judgment as a matter of law after a jury verdict, but only if the party making the motion has previously made such a motion before the case was submitted to the jury.[4] In such a case, when a motion for judgment as a matter of law is considered after a jury verdict, it is identical to the traditional motion for judgment notwithstanding the verdict. Importantly, if a party fails to make a motion for judgment as a matter of law before the case is submitted to the jury, a motion for judgment as a matter of law after the verdict (the traditional j.n.o.v.) will be unavailable.[5] Also, because the federal rules treat a post-verdict motion for judgment as a matter of law as a "renewed" motion for judgment as a matter of law, the court is limited to the arguments raised in the original motion when considering whether to grant the motion.[6]

In order to grant a motion for judgment as a matter of law, the court must determine that the party bearing the burden of proof, which is generally the plaintiff, has failed to present sufficient evidence in support of its claim. Such a failure can occur when the plaintiff simply fails to present evidence that establishes an essential element of the claim. But the court can also conclude that the plaintiff has failed to carry its burden when all the evidence

---

2. Fed. R. Civ. P. 50(a)(1).

3. Fed. R. Civ. P. 50(a)(2). The court can also impose a judgment as a matter of law *sua sponte,* without a motion, against a party at the conclusion of their case and prior to submission of the case to the jury.

4. Fed. R. Civ. P. 50(b).

5. Courts may not grant judgment as a matter of law *sua sponte* or in the absence of a renewed motion for judgment as a matter of law once a jury verdict has been issued. *See, e.g.,* Am. and Foreign Ins. Co. v. Bolt, 106 F.3d 155, 159–60 (6th Cir. 1997).

6. Fed. R. Civ. P. 50(b).

presented is so compelling that the jury would only be permitted to reach one result as a matter of law. In the latter case, courts are guided by what has come to be referred to as the substantial evidence test, which provides that a directed verdict in favor of the movant is proper unless the plaintiff has presented substantial evidence supporting its claim.

There is no clear and uniform articulation of what constitutes "substantial evidence"; however, the Supreme Court has indicated that in making these determinations courts are to consider "whether the evidence presents a sufficient disagreement to require submission to a jury or whether it is so one-sided that one party must prevail as a matter of law."[7] One court summarized the standard as follows:

> If the facts and inferences point overwhelmingly in favor of one party, such that reasonable people could not arrive at a contrary verdict, then the motion [for judgment as a matter of law] was properly granted. Conversely, if there is substantial evidence opposed to the motion such that reasonable people, in the exercise of impartial judgment, might reach differing conclusions, then such a motion was due to be denied and the case was properly submitted to the jury. . . . There must be a substantial conflict in evidence to support a jury question.[8]

The substantial evidence standard exists in opposition to the repudiated scintilla of evidence standard, which permits juries to take cases so long as the plaintiff presents any evidence, no matter how weak, in support of its claim.

In determining whether to grant a motion for judgment as a matter of law, courts are not to weigh the evidence or decide the credibility of witnesses; rather, they are to view the evidence in the light most favorable to the party opposing the motion.[9] All the evidence presented by the parties must be considered, but only

---

7. Anderson v. Liberty Lobby, Inc., 477 U.S. 242, 251–52 (1986).

8. Combs v. Plantation Patterns, 106 F.3d 1519, 1526 (11th Cir. 1997) (citation and internal quotation marks omitted).

9. Gunning v. Cooley, 281 U.S. 90 (1930); S. Atl. Ltd. P. of Tenn., L.P. v. Riese, 284 F.3d 518, 532 (4th Cir. 2002).

evidence favorable to the movant that is uncontradicted or unimpeached must be given credence by the court in evaluating the motion.[10]

Because the entry of judgment as a matter of law takes the case away from a jury and places the court in the position of deciding the case, there is an issue of whether the practice is consistent with the right to jury trial as provided for by the Seventh Amendment. The Supreme Court put this question to rest in *Galloway v. U.S.*, where it held that the Seventh Amendment does not preclude use of the directed verdict to prevent a jury from deciding a case primarily because at the time of the adoption of the amendment in 1791 there were other procedures—namely the demurrer and the new trial order—that avoided the verdict of a jury.[11]

However, the entry of judgment as a matter of law after a jury has issued a verdict does raise constitutional concerns because the Seventh Amendment provides that verdicts of juries are not reviewable.[12] Thus, under modern practice a judgment as a matter of law may only be considered as a revival of such a motion previously made rather than a new motion altogether, to preserve the legal fiction that the court is not reviewing a jury verdict but rather ruling on an earlier motion on which judgment was reserved.[13]

MOTION FOR NEW TRIAL REVIEW

Beyond the power to enter judgment as a matter of law, courts also have authority to disregard a jury's verdict and order a new trial under Federal Rule 59. Ordering that a new trial occur results in the verdict of the jury in the previous trial being thrown out and requires the parties to try the case again in front of a new jury. A

---

10. Reeves v. Sanderson Plumbing Prods., Inc., 530 U.S. 133, 151 (2000).

11. 319 U.S. 372 (1943).

12. U.S. Const., amend. VII ("[N]o fact tried by a jury, shall be otherwise re-examined in any Court of the United States, than according to the rules of the common law.").

13. Baltimore & Carolina Line, Inc. v. Redman, 295 U.S. 654 (1935).

party must make a motion for new trial within 10 days after the entry of the judgment.[14] However, courts may on their own initiative order a new trial, provided such order is issued within 10 days after the entry of judgment.[15]

To order a new trial, the court must have grounds to do so. These grounds are not listed in Rule 59, but rather the rule provides that a new trial is to be granted "for any reason for which a new trial has heretofore been granted in an action at law in federal court."[16] Some of the more common grounds relate to legal errors at trial, jury verdicts that are against the great weight of the evidence or are otherwise inappropriate, the discovery of new evidence, or the existence of improper influence on the jury.

If the judge has committed a reversible legal error at trial, such as permitting the jury to consider evidence that should have been excluded on counsel's objection, the court may order a new trial rather than require the aggrieved party to obtain a reversal and new trial order on appeal. Another example of a reversible legal error involves the judge improperly instructing the jury regarding the law. However, counsel has an obligation to point out such legal errors at trial when they occur; courts typically will not consider newly raised objections after the verdict as the basis for a new trial.

Another reason a court may order a new trial is that the jury has issued a verdict that goes against the clear weight of the evidence.[17] To make such a determination, the court weighs the evidence and considers its credibility, ordering a new trial where the court concludes that the jury has clearly reached a result that is simply wrong given the evidence. Although such weighing of the evidence clearly intrudes upon the province of the jury, because the judge is sending the case back to a new jury rather than simply resolving the matter herself, this practice has been held not to be objectionable.

---

14. FED. R. CIV. P. 59(b).

15. FED. R. CIV. P. 59(d).

16. FED. R. CIV. P. 59(a)(1)(A).

17. *See, e.g.,* United States v. Sullivan, 1 F.3d 1191, 1196 (11th Cir. 1993); Aetna Casualty & Surety Co. v. Yeats, 122 F.2d 350, 352–53 (4th Cir. 1941).

If the verdict goes against the weight of the evidence by awarding a grossly excessive verdict—one that "shocks the conscience"—the court may use *remittitur* to coax the plaintiff into settling for a lesser amount. That is, the court can threaten to grant a new trial motion if the plaintiff chooses not to accept a lower damages award identified by the judge. Rather than risk an even lower verdict or an adverse verdict before a new jury, plaintiffs often accept the reduced amount suggested by the judge. A judge in the federal system, however, may not do the converse and order the defendant to pay more than the jury has awarded or face a new trial. Even though the jury's award may be too meager in light of the evidence, the Supreme Court has held that this approach, referred to as *additur*, may not be employed by federal courts since it would result in the award of damages that a jury had not imposed.[18]

New trials may also be granted if new evidence is discovered after the jury issues its verdict. However, before doing so, courts typically will determine whether the evidence should have been discovered previously with the exercise of due diligence and whether the evidence, if considered, would make any difference in the result that the jury reached. Where evidence should have been discovered but was not due to a lack of diligence, or where the evidence does not appear to be significant enough to alter the jury's decision, courts will not order a new trial based on the newly discovered evidence.

Finally, juries or jurors can at times be improperly influenced. Improper influence over a juror or juries taints the trial in a way that undermines our faith in the verdict. Thus, where evidence of improper influence exists, a court may order a new trial before a new jury that will hopefully remain free of the same taint.

---

18.   Dimick v. Schiedt, 293 U.S. 474 (1935).

JUDGMENT AS A MATTER OF LAW & MOTION FOR NEW TRIAL CHECKLIST

With that backdrop, here is the checklist for analyzing problems presenting questions regarding motions for judgment as a matter of law or for a new trial:

A. JUDGMENT AS A MATTER OF LAW—should the court enter judgment as a matter of law?

1. **Timing**—may judgment as a matter of law be entered at this time?

a. **Close of Nonmovant's Case**—has the party against whom a judgment as a matter of law would be entered completed presentation of its evidence?

i. **No.** If not, a judgment as a matter of law would be inappropriate at this time.

ii. **Yes.** If so, proceed to the next question.

b. **Submitted to Jury?** Has the case been submitted to the jury?

i. **Yes.** If so, judgment as a matter of law may not be entered unless:

- the jury has rendered a verdict;

- a prior motion for judgment as a matter of law was made before the case was submitted to the jury; and

- the earlier motion is now being renewed. Proceed to the next question to determine whether judgment as a matter of law would be appropriate.

ii. **No.** If not, then judgment as a matter of law may be entered at this time if appropriate; proceed to the next question to determine whether judgment as a matter of law would be appropriate under the standards governing such judgments.

2. **Evidentiary Support?** Is the nonmovant's case supported by sufficient evidence such that a reasonable jury could find in favor of that party?

a. **No Evidence?** Has the nonmovant failed to present evidence establishing an essential element of their claim?

       i.   **Yes.** If so, a judgment as a matter of law against that party is appropriate.

       ii. **No.** If not, proceed to the next question to determine whether the evidence presented is sufficient.

    b. **Substantial Evidence?** Do the facts and permissible inferences point overwhelmingly in favor of one party, such that reasonable people could not arrive at a contrary verdict? In considering the facts, view the evidence in the light most favorable to the party opposing the motion and resolve all credibility issues in that party's favor.

       i.   **No.** If not, judgment as a matter of law should not be entered.

       ii. **Yes.** If so, judgment as a matter of law is appropriate and should be entered against the party failing to support its case with sufficient evidence.

B. **NEW TRIAL**—should a new trial be ordered?

  1. **Time Limit**—have 10 days passed since judgment was entered in the case?

    a. **Yes.** If so, no new trial may be ordered.

    b. **No.** If not, proceed to the next question.

  2. **Grounds**—are there grounds for ordering a new trial?

    a. **Legal Errors**—has a reversible legal error occurred?

       i.   **Yes.** If so, the court may order a new trial.

       ii. **No.** If not, proceed to the next question.

    b. **Erroneous Jury Verdict**—does the jury verdict go against the great weight of the evidence?

       i.   **Yes.** If so, the court may order a new trial.

       ii. **No.** If not, proceed to the next question.

    c. **Excessive Verdict**—is the verdict grossly excessive such that it "shocks the conscience"?

       i.   **Yes.** If so, the court may use *remittitur* to lower the awarded amount, forcing the plaintiff to accept the lower amount or face an order for a new trial.[19]

ii. **No.** If not, proceed to the next question.

d. **New Evidence**—has new evidence been discovered?

    i. **Yes.** If so, could the evidence have been discovered earlier through the exercise of due diligence?

- **Yes.** If so, the court should disregard the evidence and not order a new trial.

- **No.** If not, is the evidence material, in that it is likely to have an impact on the verdict?

    − **Yes.** If so, the court may order a new trial in light of the new evidence.

    − **No.** If not, the court should disregard the evidence and not order a new trial.

    ii. **No.** If no new evidence has been discovered, proceed to the next question.

e. **Improper Jury Influence**—has a juror or jurors been improperly influenced in such a way as to undermine our faith in the verdict as the product of impartial decision making based only on the evidence presented at trial?

    i. **Yes.** If so, the court may order a new trial.

    ii. **No.** If not, and there is no other ground for the ordering of a new trial, the court will not order a new trial.

ILLUSTRATIVE PROBLEMS

Now, here are some problems that will enable us to see how this checklist can be used to resolve questions involving judgment as a matter of law or motions for new trials:

---

19. Remember, in the face of a grossly inadequate verdict, federal courts may not use *additur* to ask defendants to accept a higher award than granted by the jury or face a new trial order.

■ PROBLEM 10.1 ■

Donna has sued Vince for negligence involving a car accident and the case is at trial. Donna's evidentiary presentation consisted of her own testimony that the light was green when she entered the intersection and therefore Vince's light must have been red. During Vince's presentation, he presents testimony of an eye witness who said that he saw that Vince's light was green when he entered the intersection. At the conclusion of Vince's presentation of his evidence Vince moves for judgment as a matter of law. The court does not grant Vince's motion.

Now, the jury has come back with a verdict in favor of Donna. Vince renews his motion for judgment as a matter of law. The court, believing that the eyewitness testimony of Vince's witness refutes Donna's claim regarding the traffic signal, reconsiders Vince's motion and enters judgment as a matter of law for Vince. Is judgment as a matter of law proper in this case?

Analysis

The first issue to consider is whether the court would be permitted to enter a judgment as a matter of law at this time. Because both parties have presented their evidence, the case has been submitted to the jury, and the jury has returned a verdict, a judgment as a matter of law can only be entered at this point if (a) a motion for judgment as a matter of law was previously made before the case was submitted to the jury at the close of all evidence, and (b) the motion is now being renewed by the movant. Here, a motion was made at the close of all evidence before submission to the jury and the motion is now being renewed. So there is no problem with the court considering this motion.

Regarding the propriety of entry of judgment as a matter of law, is Donna's case supported by sufficient evidence such that a reasonable jury could find in her favor? Viewing the evidence in the light most favorable to Donna and resolving all credibility issues in her favor, the evidence Donna presented at trial could not support a finding in her favor by a reasonable jury. Although Donna has provided her own testimony under oath that her light was green, that suggests but does not establish that Vince's signal was red. It is not direct or conclusive evidence that, if believed, establishes Vince's light was red (the lights could have malfunctioned and both signals could have been showing green). In response, Vince presented an eyewitness indicating that Vince's traffic signal was indeed green. Because Donna's evidence does not controvert this direct eyewitness testimony and she has not challenged the credibility of the witness, the court will most likely accept Vince's evidence. As a result, because Vince's evidence is entitled to be believed, no reasonable jury would be able to find that Vince was negligent in causing the accident.

■ PROBLEM 10.2 ■

Patti sued Donna for money due on a debt. At trial, Donna presented evidence that she wired money into Patti's account in the amount that she owed Patti as evidence that she already repaid the debt. Patti countered with evidence that the amount wired into her account was payment for goods unrelated to the debt at issue, and only coincidentally equaled the same amount Donna owed on the debt.

The jury returned with a verdict in favor of Donna, finding that she had paid the debt and thus was not liable to Patti for any amount. Judgment was entered for Donna and Patti moved for a new trial the next day, arguing that the jury's verdict was against the great weight of the evidence.

Should the court order a new trial?

Analysis

Patti has moved for a new trial within one day of the entry of judgment, so her motion for new trial is timely. However, she is not likely to prevail on the motion.

To order a new trial, there must be grounds to do so. Here, Patti is arguing that the jury's verdict is against the great weight of the evidence. Although Patti presented evidence indicating that Donna's payment was for the cost of goods unrelated to the debt being sued upon, the jury was entitled to disbelieve that evidence and credit Donna's assertion that the payment was indeed for the debt. Given the conflicting evidentiary presentations, with plausible claims existing on both sides, the evidence does not clearly weigh in favor of Donna or Patti. Under such circumstances, it is unlikely that a court will find that the "great weight" of the evidence goes in any particular direction. Where such is the case, a new trial is not likely to be ordered. Rather, the jury will be permitted to reach its own conclusion regarding whose testimony it will believe.

Because the verdict is not against the great weight of the evidence but rather represents the jury's reasonable choice between conflicting views of the evidence, the court should not order a new trial on this ground. Since the facts disclose no other grounds for granting a new trial, the court should not order a new trial in this case.

POINTS TO REMEMBER

- Although the court can enter a judgment as a matter of law on its own initiative prior to submitting the case to the jury, it cannot do so once a verdict has issued. Rather, it can only enter a judgment as a matter of law at that point on the motion of a party.

- A party may not seek judgment as a matter of law for the first time after a jury verdict has been issued. Parties can only renew motions made prior to submission of the case to the jury. Thus, if no prior motion has been made, judgment as a matter of law cannot be entered.

- The standard governing the entry of a judgment as a matter of law is not a clear black and white rule but an amorphous standard that refers to "substantial" or "sufficient" evidence. To apply this standard, simply try to determine whether there is a real evidentiary conflict that would permit reasonable jurors to find in favor of either party. If so, judgment as a matter of law is not proper.

- Determining whether grounds exist to support the grant of a new trial will involve the exercise of some judgment on your part. Evaluating whether a verdict is against the great weight of the evidence requires you to weigh the evidence and determine if there is a clear result the jury should have reached but did not. Similarly, your judgment is required to determine whether new evidence would impact the jury's verdict such as to warrant the ordering of a new trial.

*

CHAPTER 11

Preclusion Doctrine

C laims and issues that have previously been litigated and resolved generally are not permitted to be relitigated by parties in subsequent lawsuits. The doctrine that supplies this principle is *preclusion* doctrine. There are two strands of preclusion doctrine. The first strand is *claim preclusion*, which is also classically referred to as the doctrine of *res judicata*. The second strand of preclusion doctrine is the doctrine of *issue preclusion*, which has traditionally been known as the doctrine of *collateral estoppel*. The contours of both of these strands of preclusion doctrine will be reviewed below.

CLAIM PRECLUSION REVIEW

Claim preclusion refers to the treatment of a judgment as the full measure of relief to be accorded between the same parties on the same claim.[1] A victorious plaintiff's claim is merged into the judgment, leaving no claim to adjudicate in the future. A judgment for a defendant extinguishes the plaintiff's claim and bars a subsequent claim by the plaintiff. There are three basic requirements that must be satisfied in order for a prior adjudication to have a preclusive effect on a subsequent action.

---

1. Kaspar Wire Works, Inc. v. Leco Eng'g & Mach., Inc. 575 F.2d 530, 535 (5th Cir. 1978).

First, in order for a claim to be barred by a prior adjudication the claim at issue must fairly be considered part of the same claim as was involved in the prior suit. Thus, if the claims in the instant and prior actions are identical, this requirement is satisfied. For example, if A sues B for copyright infringement and the court enters a judgment for B, a subsequent lawsuit by A against B for the same instance of copyright infringement will be based on the identical claim that formed the basis of the initial suit. In such a case the second lawsuit would be barred by the judgment for B in the first action.

Claims need not be identical in the sense just described in order to be considered to be part of the same claim for preclusion purposes. Claims that are related to one another in the sense that they arise from the same transaction or series of connected transactions are considered part of the same claim for preclusion purposes.[2] Under the "transaction" test, all legal theories for recovery that arise from the same factual circumstances will be treated as one claim. Thus, if a claim is litigated on one theory to recover damages based on a factual occurrence no other claims arising out of those same facts will be permissible. This is the case regardless of whether the alternative legal theories are advanced (or remedies are sought) in the prior action, so long as those could have been raised in the prior action.[3]

The second requirement for claim preclusion is that the party invoking preclusion or the party against whom preclusion is being invoked must have been a party to the original action.[4] Those who were not parties to the original action can neither invoke nor be bound by the outcome of that action. However, if a party in a subsequent action was not a party to a prior action but is or was closely related to (in *privity* with) a party to the previous action, preclusion will be available to that party and to those seeking to invoke preclusion against it. That is, parties in privity with parties

---

2. RESTATEMENT (SECOND) OF JUDGMENTS § 24 (1982).

3. *See, e.g.,* Jones v. Morris Plan Bank of Portsmouth, 191 S.E. 608 (Va. 1937).

4. The parties between whom claim preclusion is being invoked must also have been adversaries in the initial action.

to the original action may invoke or be bound by claim preclusion. Privity refers to the close relationship parties may have to one another such as to indicate that the interests of one were represented by the other in the prior action. Examples include co-owners of property, successors in interest to property, or those in a relationship where one is vicariously responsible for the actions of the other.[5] Making a determination of whether parties are sufficiently related is a fact-specific inquiry that must be evaluated on a case-by-case basis.

Third and finally, only claims that have been reduced to final judgments on the merits can have a preclusive effect on subsequent claims. Any type of judgment favoring a plaintiff, whether it be a judgment entered on stipulation, a default judgment, a judgment on a jury verdict, or a summary judgment, is considered a final judgment on the merits.[6] Outcomes in favor of defendants can include judgments on the merits but preliminary dismissals that do not reach the merits such as dismissals for lack of jurisdiction, improper venue, or failure to join a party under Rule 19 may not be treated as judgments on the merits unless otherwise indicated. Generally speaking, if the court's final ruling is based on the substance of the claim rather than a technical procedural ground, the ruling will be regarded as a final judgment on the merits.[7]

In sum, claim preclusion operates to bar relitigation of claims between the same or closely related parties where the current claim is transactionally related to the earlier claim and the prior action resulted in a final judgment on the merits.

ISSUE PRECLUSION REVIEW

Collateral estoppel or issue preclusion, as it is now referred to, is a doctrine that bars the relitigation of issues that were actually

---

5. *See* RESTATEMENT (SECOND) OF JUDGMENTS, § 75 (1982).

6. GENE R. SHREVE & PETER RAVEN–HANSEN, UNDERSTANDING CIVIL PROCEDURE 505 (3d ed. 2002).

7. JACK FRIEDENTHAL, MARY KAY KANE & ARTHUR MILLER, CIVIL PROCEDURE § 14.7

(West's Hornbook Series) (4th ed. 2005). There are many complications and nuances to the final judgment rule that are too varied to go into here. Students should consult Friedenthal, Kane and Miller, § 14.7 for a further, more in-depth discussion of this aspect of claim preclusion.

litigated in a prior action, provided the adjudication of those issues was essential to the judgment. Issue preclusion differs from claim preclusion in several important respects. First, issue preclusion applies to issues not claims; thus, the subsequent action can involve a completely different, unrelated claim and collateral estoppel can still apply. What matters for collateral estoppel is whether the issue raised in subsequent litigation is the same as an issue litigated in prior litigation, not the sameness of claims. Second, while res judicata can bar claims that were not raised because those claims could and should have been raised in the first action, collateral estoppel can only prevent the relitigation of issues actually raised in the prior action. Despite these differences, the policy behind the doctrines is the same: to promote finality and repose and to prevent duplicative litigation.

When issue preclusion applies, the previous determination of that issue is treated as conclusive and binding in the subsequent action. For example, assume that *A* sues *B* for breach of contract for failure to make a payment due and for failure to complete a required task. *B* contests the validity of the contract and denies having breached any contract that may exist. The court finds that a valid contract exists between *A* and *B* but concludes that *B* only breached the contract by failing to make a payment due. In a subsequent action on that contract involving a new alleged breach of the contract by *B*, *B* would not be permitted to relitigate the validity of the contract because that issue was already litigated in an earlier suit between *A* and *B*.

There are four general requirements for collateral estoppel to apply as a bar to the relitigation of an issue. First, as with claim preclusion, for issue preclusion to apply the parties involved must be identical to (or in privity with) those involved in the prior action. Although this is the general rule, it is possible for one who was not a party to the prior action to invoke issue preclusion against an adversary in a subsequent action based on the fact that the adversary fully litigated and lost that issue previously. Such use of issue preclusion is referred to as *nonmutual collateral estoppel*.[8]

Second, the issue raised in the prior action must be identical to the issue raised in the subsequent action. This identity-of-issues requirement is narrower than the identity-of-claims requirement for claim preclusion. Similar or transactionally related issues will not preclude one another. As the Supreme Court put it in ***Commissioner of Internal Revenue v. Sunnen***: "[C]ollateral estoppel . . . must be confined to situations where the matter raised in the second suit is identical in all respects with that decided in the first proceeding. . . ."[9] Presenting new facts or raising new legal arguments will not enable a party to overcome the preclusive effect of a prior determination where issue preclusion is found to apply. What is important is that the same issue is involved in both actions, and new evidence or novel legal theories do not alter the fact that the issues are the same.

Third, the issue must have been actually litigated and determined in the prior action. This basically means that the parties must have fought over the issue, presenting conflicting positions and litigating to an adjudicated determination on the issue. Thus, issues embodied in judgments entered by consent or default would not receive issue preclusive effect because the issues were not actually litigated but rather were simply determined.[10] Where an issue was not actually raised and litigated by the parties in the prior action, issue preclusion will not apply.

Finally, for the prior determination of an issue to have preclusive effect, resolution of the issue in question must have been necessary to the judgment reached in the earlier case. The rationale for this requirement is that if the determination was not essential to the judgment entered, the party losing on the issue may have had insufficient incentive to litigate the issue fully and

---

8. Standefer v. United States, 447 U.S. 10, 21 (1980) (citing Blonder–Tongue Labs., Inc. v. Univ. of Ill. Found., 402 U.S. 313 (1971)).

9. 333 U.S. 591 (1948).

10. Arizona v. California, 530 U.S. 392 (2000).

vigorously. This requirement insures that the issue will have truly been disputed by the parties because real disputes can be expected over issues that matter to the outcome of the case. One is able to determine whether an issue was necessary to the judgment by asking whether a different decision regarding the issue would have affected the outcome of the case; if not, the issue was not necessary to the judgment and will not have preclusive effect.[11] If it is unclear whether the determination of an issue was necessary to the outcome of the case, no preclusive effect can be given to the issue. This can happen, for example, where a general verdict is issued based on evidence presenting multiple possible grounds supporting recovery.[12]

 PRECLUSION DOCTRINE CHECKLIST

Here is the checklist for analyzing problems presenting questions regarding preclusive effect:

A. CLAIM PRECLUSION—is the claim barred by a prior adjudication?

  1. Same Claim? Is the current claim the same as a claim raised in the prior action?

  a. **Identical Claims**—are the claims exactly identical?

  i. **Yes.** If so, the claims in both actions are the same; proceed to Part A.2.

  ii. **No.** If not, proceed to the next question.

  b. **Transactionally Related Claims**—do the claims arise out of the same transaction or series of connected transactions?

---

11. *See, e.g.,* Rios v. Davis, 373 S.W.2d 386 (Tex. Civ. App. 1963) (holding that a finding of a plaintiff's contributory negligence in prior action rendered finding of defendant's negligence in the same action unnecessary to the outcome and thus not entitled to issue preclusive effect).

12. Russell v. Place, 94 U.S. 606 (1876) (general verdict entered on multiple allegations of infringement prevented giving issue preclusive effect to prior judgment).

i.   **Yes.** If so, the claims in both actions are the same, proceed to Part A.2.

    ii.   **No.** If not, the claims are not sufficiently identical to grant preclusive effect to the earlier adjudication.

2.   **Same Parties?** Does the current action involve the same parties that were parties to and adversaries in the original action?

    a.   **Identical Parties**—are the parties in both actions identical?

        i.   **Yes.** If so, then the identity-of-parties requirement is satisfied. Proceed to Part A.3.

        ii.   **No.** If not, then proceed to the next question.

    b.   **Parties in Privity**—if a party in the current action was not a party to the original action, is there a relationship between that party and a party in the original action that warrants treating the non-party to the initial action as if it were a party?

        i.   **Substantive Relationship**—is there a substantive legal relationship that unifies the interests of the non-party and the party to the initial action?

            •   **No.** If not, then proceed to the next question.

            •   **Yes.** If so, the identity-of-parties requirement is satisfied. Proceed to Part A.3.

        ii.   **Representation in Prior Action**—was the nonparty represented in the prior action by a party to the initial action?

            •   **No.** If not, the identity-of-parties requirement is not satisfied.

            •   **Yes.** If so, the identity-of-parties requirement is satisfied. Proceed to Part A.3.

3.   **Final Judgment?** Was the prior action concluded by a final judgment on the merits? Generally speaking, a judgment is treated as on the merits if it is based on the validity of the claims at issue in the case rather than on procedural grounds.

    a.   **Yes.** If so, the resolution is considered a final judgment on the merits. The judgment may have preclusive effect if all the previous requirements have been satisfied.

b. **No.** if the case was resolved on procedural grounds, such as lack of jurisdiction, improper venue, or failure to join a party under Rule 19, the resolution of the case does not constitute a final judgment on the merits and no preclusive effect may be given to the prior action.

B. ISSUE PRECLUSION—has an issue already been conclusively resolved between the parties in a prior action?

1. **Same Parties?** Does the current action involve the same parties that were parties to and adversaries in the original action? *See supra* Part A.2 for the steps in this analysis.[13]

   a. **Yes.** If so, proceed to the next question.

   b. **No.** If not, then issue preclusion is not appropriate.

2. **Same Issue?** Is the issue raised in the prior action identical in all respects to the issue raised in the current action?

   a. **Yes.** If so, proceed to the next question.

   b. **No.** If not, then issue preclusion is not appropriate.

3. **Actually Litigated and Determined?** Was the issue actually litigated and determined in the prior action, meaning the issue was raised and argued by the parties?

   a. **Yes.** If so, proceed to the next question.

   b. **No.** If not, then issue preclusion is not appropriate.

4. **Necessary to the Judgment?** Was resolution of the issue in question necessary to the judgment reached in the case?

   a. **Outcome Determinative**—would a different decision regarding the issue have affected the outcome of the case?

      i. **Yes.** If so, the determination of the issue was necessary to the judgment and it should be given preclusive effect in the subsequent action.

      ii. **No.** If not, the determination of the issue was not necessary to the judgment and it should not be given preclusive effect in the subsequent action.

---

13. Remember, however, that nonmutual collateral estoppel is a possibility, provided the party to be bound had the opportunity to litigate the issue fully in the prior action and lost.

iii. **Unclear.** If it is unclear whether it would have made a difference, refer to the next question.

b. **Multiple Grounds**—is it unclear on which of multiple grounds for relief a judgments relies?

i. **Yes.** If so, then no preclusive effect may be given to the prior determination.

ii. **No.** If it is clear on which ground or grounds the judgment relies, the determination of those issues are to be given preclusive effect.

ILLUSTRATIVE PROBLEMS

Now, here are some problems that will enable us to see how this checklist can be used to resolve preclusive effect questions:

■ PROBLEM 11.1 ■

Donald sued the City of Martindale in Emporia state court for money due on a contract to construct federally subsidized low-income housing. The jury returned a verdict for Martindale and judgment was entered against Donald.

Donald has now gone to federal court in Emporia and brought suit against Martindale under the Federal Housing Construction Act, which entitles contractors doing work on federal housing to sue localities administering the construction project for money due on housing construction contracts.

Martindale asserts the Emporia state court verdict as res judicata against the federal action. Result?

Analysis

In order for a prior adjudication to have res judicata preclusive effect on a subsequent action, the previous action must have involved the same claim between the same parties and must have ended in a final judgment on the merits.

Here, the first question is whether the federal action involves the same claim as was involved in the initial state court action. Although the federal action seeks recovery based on federal law, the action arises from the same facts as did Donald's claim in the original state court action. Both cases arose out of Martindale's alleged debt to Donald for construction work. The mere fact that the cases involve two different legal theories is not relevant; what matters is that the two claims are transactionally related. Similarly, it makes no difference that Donald did not assert the federal claim in the initial action; the fact that he could have raised it but did not results in it being waived if a final judgment is entered. Thus, these two actions involve the same claim and satisfy the first requirement for claim preclusion.

The second and third requirements are easily satisfied here. The parties in both actions are identical so the same parties requirement is met. Also, the previous case ended in a verdict for the defendant, which is a final judgment on the merits.

Because all three requirements for claim preclusion are satisfied here, the court should dismiss the federal action on the ground that it is barred by the prior action in state court.

■ PROBLEM 11.2 ■

Harold sues James in Orange County court for trespassing on Greenacre, an investment property that Harold owns but has never occupied. James argues that Harold does not own Greenacre and that if he does, James did not trespass on it. The jury returns a verdict in favor of Harold, finding that Harold indeed was the owner of Greenacre and that James trespassed on it.

The following month, James brings an ejectment action against Harold in Los Angeles County court to get Harold kicked off of Greenacre (after the Orange County suit, Harold decided to move onto Greenacre). James claims that he is and has been the true owner of Greenacre by virtue of a quitclaim deed Harold gave to James after a poker game several years ago.

Harold asserts the prior determination of his ownership in the Orange County action as collateral estoppel against the relitigation of the issue of ownership in the present action.

Should the court enter a judgment in favor of Harold on the basis of collateral estoppel?

Analysis

Collateral estoppel only applies to issues that were actually litigated and necessary to the judgment in an earlier action between the same parties. So first we ask if the second action involves the same parties as were involved in the first. The answer is yes; both actions involve Harold and James, although their roles as plaintiff and defendant have been reversed.

Second, we ask whether the issue being raised in the second action is identical to an issue raised in the initial action. Again the answer is yes; the issue of Harold's ownership, which is being raised now was also raised in the first action.

Third, we want to know whether the issue of Harold's ownership was actually litigated and determined in the first action. The facts indicate that James raised Harold's lack of ownership as a defense to the trespass claim being asserted against him. Harold obviously asserted his own ownership as the basis for his claim of trespass. Further, the jury's verdict explicitly found that Harold was indeed the owner of Greenacre. Thus, the issue was actually litigated and determined in the initial action.

Finally, we have to figure out whether the determination of the issue was necessary to the outcome of the first case. An essential component of finding James liable to Harold for trespass is that Harold owned the property in question. Had the jury determined otherwise, that Harold did not own the property, the outcome would have been different; James could not be liable to Harold for trespassing on property that Harold did not own. Thus, determination of the issue was necessary to the outcome of the first case.

Having satisfied each of the requirements for issue preclusion, the court should find that the prior determination of Harold's ownership is conclusive and binding on the parties and precludes relitigation of that issue in the suit brought in Los Angeles County court. A judgment for Harold should be entered as a result.

POINTS TO REMEMBER

- Claims need not be identical in order for claim preclusion to apply. If the claims are transactionally related or arise out of a series of connected transactions, the earlier claim can bar relitigation of the subsequent claim (provided the other requirements for claim preclusion are satisfied).

- For issue preclusion, however, the issues raised in the previous and current actions must be identical; transactionally related issues will not suffice.

- While the doctrine of issue preclusion requires that the issue have been actually litigated, there is no similar requirement for claim preclusion. For claim preclusion to apply, the current claim can be one that could have been raised in the prior action but was not.

- Generally, the same parties must be involved in the current action as were involved in the prior action for the previous action to be given claim preclusive effect. However, a nonparty to the earlier action may be bound if she is in privity with a party to the prior action.

- The same principles hold for issue preclusion, except that a nonparty to the earlier action not in privity with a party to the prior action may invoke issue preclusion in the current action if their adversary fully litigated and lost on that issue previously (nonmutual collateral estoppel).

Conclusion: General Examination Tips

Now that you have the full set of checklists for each of the topics that you will be grappling with on your examination, there are some final bits of advice to help you ace your civil procedure examination:

Before the Examination

- Prepare early for examinations by reviewing information learned as you go along rather than awaiting the end of the semester.

- Review the material by working on as many hypothetical problems as you are able to tackle. It is important to gain experience answering and writing out answers to problems before the examination.

- Meet with your professor regularly to gain useful insight into what he or she feels is important about particular topics and to develop a deeper understanding of the material. This time can also be used to obtain information regarding what type of analysis the professor expects on an examination.

- Synthesize the material early on by seeing the connections between different topics covered within the course to develop a more comprehensive, holistic view of the material.

- Do not neglect information regarding the policy underpinnings or implications of various legal rules learned in the course. These policy issues become important in equipping students with the ability to resolve tough questions and to provide rationales for particular legal outcomes.

- Do not rely on a mere mastery of the substantive material to develop a sense of preparedness for the exam. What is equally important is a deep *understanding* of the material—both rules and policy—which will enable you to engage in higher-level analysis of the problems that you will face on the exam.

During the Examination

- Before writing a response to a question, outline the answer to facilitate your ability to provide a clear, organized response and to structure your thinking about the question in a way that will help to ensure that the answer covers all of the issues that need to be addressed.

- On the exam, law professors are not simply looking for students to be able to apply the law they have been taught to a given set of facts to achieve a result. In addition to demonstrating such ability, superior exam takers demonstrate a depth of understanding beyond the black-letter law that animates their discussion of the issues throughout an exam. The recognition of difficult questions and reference to an array of underlying policies to arrive at a resolution is the mark of a good answer.

- Always identify your assumptions. If you are assuming certain facts as the basis for your answer, make those assumptions explicit.

- Never give a simple conclusion regarding the proper result as your answer to a question on an exam. Provide a full explanation showing your analysis. On law school exams the journey is much more important than the destination.

- Rather than simply reaching a particular result because a certain rule or case calls for that result, reason toward a conclusion by identifying key facts in the question, similar facts in other relevant cases, and any policy issues that support the outcome you intend to reach.

- Regardless of how difficult or inconclusive the question may seem, an answer to an examination question must reach a result. Do not equivocate by responding that on the one hand X and on the other hand Y. Use legal judgment, reasoning, and analysis to identify a superior position and provide arguments for your choice.

- Consider the arguments on both sides of an issue and state them. Then take the opportunity to apply your understanding of the principles and policies involved as well as any relevant precedent to side with a particular result.

- When deciding between two competing rules or approaches to resolving an issue, clearly state which approach you intend to apply and articulate the arguments for why that is the better approach.

- First-year law school examinations are typically competitive affairs in the sense that one's performance is evaluated based on the performance of others. Thus, simply knowing the material and properly applying the law to facts will not be enough since fellow students are capable of the same. Distinguish yourself by going the extra mile through engaging in an analysis that demonstrates depth of knowledge and true understanding rather than rote memorization or dexterity with available source material (for open-book exams).

- In addition to the quality of one's answer, make sure to provide an answer that is comprehensive in that it identifies all of the issues raised in the question. Working on practice questions is a good way to develop the ability to spot issues, making it critical that one work with practice questions prior to the exam.

After the Examination

It's over! Don't waste time talking with other classmates about the exam. You'll just create more anxiety for yourself. Focus on the next exam; or, if civil procedure is your last exam, celebrate being done!

———————

I truly hope the above material will be helpful to you as you go through your civil procedure course and examination. Acing civil procedure is not difficult with the right amount of study and preparation; these checklists should help you clearly organize procedural doctrines in a way that will make them manageable and facilitate your application of the doctrines to particular fact patterns. Good luck!

APPENDIX:

Mini–Checklists

In this Appendix students will find truncated, one- to three-page versions of the checklists for each topic, for quick reference and use when it is necessary to be able to find something quickly under a time crunch during an exam. These reduced versions cover the key points that need to be checked in your analysis. Proper use and understanding of these "mini-checklists" requires a complete understanding of the full checklists presented in the main text of this book.

PERSONAL JURISDICTION

A. FEDERAL OR STATE COURT? If in federal court, state jurisdictional limits apply unless alternate basis for jurisdiction is provided for in Rules 4(k).

B. LONG-ARM STATUTE—does the state's long-arm statute authorize personal jurisdiction under these facts?

C. CONSTITUTIONAL ANALYSIS—does the assertion of jurisdiction satisfy the requirements of Due Process?

1. **Traditional Bases for Personal Jurisdiction.** Is one of the traditional bases for personal jurisdiction applicable?

   a. In-state service

   b. Voluntary Appearance/Waiver

   c. Consent

   d. Family Status

   e. Nonresident Plaintiffs

   f. State Citizens

2. **Does the assertion of jurisdiction satisfy the minimum contacts standard of *Int'l Shoe*?**

   a. **Continuous & Systematic and Related Contacts—** personal jurisdiction is appropriate.

   b. **Continuous & Systematic but Unrelated**—possible situation permitting general jurisdiction. Contacts must be "substantial."

   c. **Single & Isolated and Unrelated**—no personal jurisdiction.

   d. **Single & Isolated and Related**—possible specific jurisdiction.

3. **Specific Jurisdiction Analysis**—can specific jurisdiction be exercised over the defendant?

a. **Minimum Contacts**—are there minimum contacts between the defendant and the forum state?

   i.   Purposeful Availment

   ii. Intentional Torts

   iii. Contract-plus

   iv. Stream of Commerce

   v. Internet Cases

   vi. *In Rem* Actions

b. **Reasonableness**—would the exercise of jurisdiction be (un)reasonable?

   i.   Burden to the defendant

   ii. State interest

   iii. Plaintiff's interest in obtaining relief

   iv. Interstate judicial system's interest in efficient resolution of controversies

   v. Shared interest of the States in furthering fundamental substantive social policies

NOTICE AND THE OPPORTUNITY TO BE HEARD

A. NOTICE—Was notice reasonably calculated, under all the circumstances, to apprise interested parties of the pendency of the action and afford them an opportunity to present their objections?

   1. **Adequate Information**—does the notice convey sufficient information to notify the party of how and by when it should respond?

   2. **Timeliness**—does the notice allow reasonable time to appear?

   3. **Method**—is the method of giving notice a method that one desirous of actually informing the party might reasonably adopt to achieve actual notice? Was the most reasonable means available employed?

      a. **No.** If there is a better means that is available and reasonably practical, then it should be employed.

      b. **Yes.** Where a superior method exists but is too expensive, time consuming, or burdensome, then it need not be employed over more practical methods under *Mullane*.

B. OPPORTUNITY TO BE HEARD—does the pre-deprivation hearing comport with the constitutional requirements of due process?

   1. **Property Interest at Stake**—what is the nature of the defendant's property interest at stake?

   2. **Risk of Erroneous Deprivation**—what is the risk that the defendant will be wrongfully deprived of its property?

      a. **Showing**—what type of showing does the plaintiff have to make?

      b. **Bond**—is there a bond requirement?

      c. **Judge**—is the decision made by a judge or a non-judicial court official such as a clerk?

3. **Plaintiff's Interest**—what is the interest of the party seeking the prejudgment remedy and if relevant, any ancillary interest of the government?

SUBJECT MATTER JURISDICTION

A. ORIGINAL FEDERAL COURT JURISDICTION—is there original jurisdiction over the claim by the plaintiff?

1. Diversity Jurisdiction—are the requirements of 28 U.S.C. § 1332 satisfied?

    a. **Diverse Parties**—are the parties diverse under § 1332?

        i. Citizens of different states or State citizen versus an alien

        ii. Citizens of different states with aliens as additional parties

        iii. A foreign state versus a state citizen

    b. **Complete Diversity**—is there complete diversity?

    c. **Amount in Controversy**—is the claim for more than $75,000?

        i. Punitives included; costs and pre-judgment interest excluded.

        ii. *Aggregation*—multiple claims by plaintiff against single defendant can be aggregated; claims alleging joint & several liability against multiple defendants are valued based on the entire amount claimed.

2. Federal Question Jurisdiction—§ 1331 or other provision:

    a. **Essential Federal Element**

        i. *Creation Test*—is the claim created by federal law?

        ii. *Substantial Federal Interest Test*—does the claim depend upon application or interpretation of federal law? Substantial? Would jurisdiction disturb any congressionally approved balance of federal and state responsibilities?

    b. **Well-Pleaded Complaint Rule**—does the essential federal element appear on the face of plaintiff's well-pleaded complaint?

B. SUPPLEMENTAL JURISDICTION—28 U.S.C. § 1367:

    1. **1367(a)**—is there a claim over which the court has original jurisdiction (see above analysis)? If so, is the supplemental claim at issue based on the same common nucleus of operative fact?

    2. **1367(b)**—does § 1367(b) bar supplemental jurisdiction in this case?

        a. Diversity sole basis for court's jurisdiction? *and* either

        b. Supplemental claim by plaintiff against parties joined under Rule 14, 19, 20, or 24? *or*

        c. Diversity sole basis for jurisdiction and claim by a plaintiff joined under Rule 19 or 24?

    3. **Discretionary Basis for Denial of Jurisdiction?**

        a. Novel or complex state issue?

        b. State claim substantially predominates?

        c. Federal claims have been dismissed?

        d. Other exceptional circumstances?

C. REMOVAL JURISDICTION—basis for removing claims to federal court?

    1. Original jurisdiction over plaintiff's claims?

    2. Defendant seeking to remove for diversity cannot be from forum state.

    3. 30–day time limit and defendant unanimity.

VENUE

A. WAIVER—has the party challenging venue waived the challenge?

   1. Forum Selection Clause

   2. Failure to Object

B. SPECIAL VENUE STATUTE—is there a special venue statute that applies, such as the alien venue provision, 28 U.S.C. § 1391(d)? If so, then venue must be evaluated under the special provision, not the general venue provisions of § 1391.

C. GENERAL VENUE STATUTE—if no waiver has occurred and no special venue statute applies, then apply the general venue statute (28 U.S.C. § 1391).

   1. Do all the defendants reside within the same state?

      a. Identify the residency of each defendant.

         i. *Individuals*—residency is equated with citizenship (domicile).

         ii. *Corporations*—resident in districts where they are subject to personal jurisdiction.

      b. If all defendants reside in the same state, venue is proper in a district where any of the defendants reside.

   2. Is there a district where events creating claim took place or where property that is the subject of the action is located? If so, venue is proper there.

   3. Fallback Provision—if no proper venue can be identified based on the first two tests, then determine venue with reference to the fallback provisions of the statute.

      a. Diversity Cases—venue is proper in the district where any defendant is subject to personal jurisdiction.

      b. Non-Diversity Cases—venue is proper in district where any defendant can be found.

D. TRANSFER OF VENUE—is the transfer being made to a court where the action could have been brought initially? If so, transfer is okay.

E. FORUM NON CONVENIENS—have the two prerequisites for a dismissal for forum non conveniens been met?

   1. Adequate Alternate Forum—is there a forum outside of the current court system that is available for the prosecution of plaintiff's claim?

   2. Public and Private Interests—do private and public interests weigh in favor of having the case heard in the alternate venue?

   a. **Private Interest Factors**—location of the events giving rise to the case; availability of compulsory process for attendance of the unwilling; ability to implead other parties in the court; ability to take a view of premises involved in the dispute; ease and cost of access to sources of proof; and enforceability of a judgment if one is obtained.

   b. **Public Interest Factors**—whether the dispute involves local people or events; whether the dispute is likely to be decided under local law.

ERIE DOCTRINE

A. DIVERSITY ACTION—is this a diversity action? *Erie* doctrine is an issue principally in diversity cases.

B. CONTROLLING FEDERAL RULE OR STATUTE—is there a federal rule or statute that is sufficiently broad to control the issue before the court?

    1. Not Controlling—in the absence of a controlling federal rule or statute, move to the *Erie* analysis below.

    2. Controlling—if the federal rule or statute is controlling of the issue before the court, proceed with the *Hanna* Rules Enabling Act analysis.

C. *HANNA* RULES ENABLING ACT ANALYSIS

    1. Direct Conflict—is the applicable federal rule or statute in "direct collision" with the law of the relevant state?

    2. Constitutionality of the Federal Rule or Statute—does the rule or statute regulate matters that are procedural or capable of being classified as either substantive or procedural?

    3. Compliance with the Rules Enabling Act—if a Federal Rule is at issue, does the rule comply with the Rules Enabling Act, meaning it regulates procedure and does not "abridge, enlarge or modify" any substantive right?

D. *ERIE* ANALYSIS—if no valid federal statute or Rule covers the issue before the court, then the question becomes whether the federal practice in question or the conflicting state practice should be applied.

    1. Substance v. Procedure Test—can the issue be readily labeled as substantive and thus beyond the scope of federal courts to regulate within states?

    2. *Hanna*'s Modified Outcome-Determinative Test—would application of the federal standard implicate the "twin aims" of *Erie*?

    a.   Promote forum shopping?

    b.   Result in "substantial" variations between outcomes in state and federal courts?

3. *Byrd* **Balancing Approach**—outcome determinativeness must be evaluated against the substantive policy interests furthered by the respective state and federal practices.

    a.   **State Substantive Policy Furthered?** Is the state practice "bound up with the definition of the rights and obligations of the parties," such that the practice furthers some substantive state policy?

    b.   **Countervailing Federal Interest?** Does the federal practice promote an important federal substantive policy interest that outweighs the significance of the state policy underlying the state practice?

PLEADINGS

A. ADEQUACY OF THE COMPLAINT—is the complaint sufficient under the Federal Rules?

1. **Jurisdiction**—does the complaint allege subject matter jurisdiction? Rule 8(a)(1).

2. **Claim**—does the complaint adequately state a claim showing that the pleader is entitled to relief? Rule 8(a)(2).

    a. **Special Matters**—if the pleading alleges fraud or mistake it must specify the circumstances constituting fraud or mistake. Rule 9(b).

    b. **All Other Claims**—does the pleading allege facts showing plausible entitlement to relief?

        i. Is *D* given enough to understand *P*'s allegations?

        ii. Does the claim as pleaded, if true, entitle *P* to relief?

3. **Damages**—adequate prayer for judgment and relief? Rule 8(a)(3).

    a. **Special Damages**—are the damages the foreseeable result of injuries or events mentioned in the complaint? If not, they should be specifically stated. Rule 9(g).

    b. **Permissible Award**—the final judgment can grant all relief to which the party is entitled based on the evidence, except that relief granted on a default judgment may not exceed the prayer.

B. ADEQUACY OF THE ANSWER—is the answer sufficient under the Rules?

1. **Denials**—are the defendant's denials sufficient to deny properly the averments made in the complaint? Rule 8(b).

    a. **General Denial**—is there any portion of the allegations that were generally denied that are manifestly true or that the denying party knew was true when they denied it? If so, the general denial will be ineffective and the allegations will be deemed admitted.

b. **Lack of Information**—if the answer pleads a lack of information, is the matter presumptively within the party's knowledge? If so, the response is ineffective and the allegation will be admitted.

2. **Affirmative Defenses**—if a defendant seeks to introduce evidence pertaining to an affirmative defense, the question will be, "Has the defendant sufficiently pleaded the defense in its answer?" Rule 8(c).

C. AMENDMENTS—is the proposed amendment proper under the Rules?

1. **Amendment as a Matter of Course**—if a responsive pleading is permitted but not yet filed, or if 20 days have not passed when no responsive pleading is allowed, the party may amend its pleading without permission of the court.

2. **Amendment Not as a Matter of Course**—an amendment can be obtained with consent of the adverse party or permission of the court. The court is to grant amendments freely unless:

a. There is evidence of bad faith, or

b. There is evidence of substantial unfair prejudice.

3. **Amendment to Conform to the Evidence**—if the amendment seeks to conform a pleading to evidence presented or sought to be presented at trial, such an amendment should be permitted if:

a. **Consent**—there is either express or implied (no objection) consent to trying issues not raised in or relevant to the pleadings.

b. **Leave of the Court**—a motion to amend to conform is granted unless the objecting party would be prejudiced.

D. RELATION BACK OF AMENDMENTS—if an amendment is proper and has been allowed, does it relate back to the time of filing?

    1. **Statute of Limitations Law**—does the law providing the statute of limitations for the action permit relation back? Rule 15(c)(1)(A).

    2. **Amendment Involving Claim or Defense**—if the amendment involves a claim or defense, does it arise out of the same transaction or occurrence set forth in the original pleading? Rule 15(c)(1)(B).

    3. **Amendment Involving a New Party**—if the amendment seeks to change the party against whom a claim is asserted, ask these questions:

        a. **Satisfaction of Rule 15(c)(1)(B)**—are the requirements of Rule 15(c)(1)(B) satisfied? See analysis *supra* at Part D.2.

        b. **Notice**—did the party to be brought into the action receive, within 120 days, notice of the institution of the action such that it will not be prejudiced in mounting a defense on the merits?

        e. **Awareness of Real Party Status**—did the new party know that but for a mistake it would have been named in the suit?

E. RULE 11—are sanctions under Rule 11 appropriate in this case?

    1. **Violation of Rule 11?** Has there been a violation of Rule 11?

        a. **Pre-Filing Inquiry**—did the attorney signing the filing conduct a reasonable pre-filing inquiry?

        b. **Improper Purpose**—has the filing been made for an improper purpose, such as harassment, delay, or to increase costs?

        c. **Frivolous Legal Arguments**—are the legal contentions made in the filing supported by the law or by a nonfrivolous argument for the "extension, modification, or reversal of existing law?"

d. **Unsupportable Factual Allegations**—do the factual allegations or denials have (or are likely to have) evidentiary support?

2. **Sanctions**—given a violation, can the court impose sanctions?

a. **Motion**—if a motion for sanctions under Rule 11 has been made, ask:

i. Have 21 days passed since the motion was served on the adverse party?

ii. If so, has the adverse party withdrawn the challenged filing?

b. **On Court's Initiative**—has the court directed the attorney to show cause why it has not violated Rule 11(b)? If so and if the court finds that Rule 11 has been violated, it may enter sanctions.

JOINDER

A. **PERMISSIBILITY OF THE CLAIM**—is the claim permissible?

1. **Claim Already Asserted**—if the claimant has already successfully asserted a claim against the party, additional claims may be joined with that claim under Rule 18(a).

2. **Defending Party's Claim against Opposing Party.** If the claim is being asserted by a defending party against its opponent, it may be asserted as a counterclaim.

   a. **Compulsory Counterclaim**—if the claim arises out of the same transaction or occurrence as the claim asserted against the claimant, the claim must be asserted or it will be waived.

   b. **Permissive Counterclaim**—if not, the claim is permissive and may be brought at the counterclaimant's option.

3. **Claim against Non-Aggressor.** If the claim is not made by a defendant against an opponent, whom is the claim being asserted against?

   a. **Coparty**—a claim against a coparty may be asserted as a crossclaim under Rule 13(g) if it arises out of the same transaction or occurrence as the original claim or counterclaim or asserts derivative liability.

   b. **Third-Party Defendant by the Plaintiff (or vice versa)**—if the claim arises out of the same transaction or occurrence as the plaintiff's claim against the defendant it may be asserted under Rule 14.

   c. **Rule 19 or 24 Party**—determine the party's status in the lawsuit once joined and apply the relevant analysis from above.

B. **PERMISSIVE PARTY JOINDER.** Is the joinder of a party permissible?

1. **Joinder of Defendants**—if the plaintiff is asserting against the defendants a right to relief arising out of the same

transaction or occurrence and involving a common question of law or fact, the plaintiff may join the defendants in a single action under Rule 20(a).

2. **Joinder of Plaintiffs**—if the plaintiffs are asserting a right to relief arising out of the same transaction or occurrence and involving a common question of law or fact, the plaintiffs may join in a single action under Rule 20(a).

3. **Joinder of Nonparties**—if the party seeking joinder is a defending party, she may implead a non-party into the action as a Rule 14 third-party defendant if the party is alleging that the non-party is liable for all or part of the plaintiff's claim against the defending party.

4. **Joinder by Nonparties**—if the party seeking joinder is a non-party, they may intervene under either of the following two circumstances:

   a. **Intervention of Right**—a non-party has a right to intervene under Rule 24(a)(2) if:

      i. The nonparty has an interest in the action,

      ii. That would be impaired by resolution of the action, and

      iii. *Provided* the nonparty's interests are not adequately represented by existing parties.

   b. **Permissive Intervention**—if the nonparty does not have a right to intervene under Rule 24(a)(2), it may be permitted to intervene under Rule 24(b)(1) if the non-party's claim or defense and the main action have a question of law or fact in common.

C. **COMPULSORY PARTY JOINDER.** Must a nonparty be joined in an action?

   1. **Necessity.** Is the absentee a necessary party under Rule 19(a)? The party is necessary if one of the following statements is true:

a. **Availability of Complete Relief**—in the nonparty's absence, the court would be unable to afford complete relief among those who are already parties to the action.

b. **Impairment to Absentee's Claimed Interest**—disposition of the action in the nonparty's absence would impair or impede the nonparty's ability to protect their claimed interest relating to the subject of the action.

c. **Threat to Existing Parties**—disposition of the action in the nonparty's absence would leave existing parties subject to a substantial risk of incurring multiple or inconsistent obligations.

2. **Feasibility of Joinder**—if a nonparty is deemed to be a necessary party, is their joinder in the action feasible?

a. **Personal Jurisdiction**—can the court obtain personal jurisdiction over the necessary party?

b. **Subject Matter Jurisdiction**—will the joinder of the party deprive the court of subject matter jurisdiction over the action?

c. **Venue**—has the necessary party objected to venue and if so, is venue proper?

3. **Indispensability of the Party**—if joinder of the necessary party is not feasible, should the court dismiss the action in the party's absence? Four factors must be balanced using "equity and good conscience":

a. **Prejudice?** To what extent would a judgment in the necessary party's absence prejudice that party or the existing parties?

b. **Lessening of Prejudice?** Can the prejudice to existing parties or the necessary party be lessened or avoided through protective provisions in the judgment, the shaping of relief, or other measures?

c. **Adequacy of Remedy?** Will the judgment rendered in the absence of the necessary party be adequate?

d. **Adequate Remedy Elsewhere?** If the action is dismissed, will the plaintiff have an adequate remedy?

DISCOVERY

A. DISCOVERABILITY—is the material requested discoverable under the Federal Rules?

    1. Relevance—is the material relevant to a claim or defense of any party in the action? The material need not be admissible at trial.

    2. Limitations—do circumstances exist that require the court to limit discovery of the material in question?

        a. **Duplicative**—is the requested material unreasonably cumulative or duplicative of material already sought and received?

        b. **Less Burdensome Alternative**—is the requested material obtainable from some other source that is more convenient, less burdensome, or less expensive?

        c. **Missed Opportunity**—has the requesting party had ample opportunity by discovery to obtain the information sought?

        d. **Cost Surpasses Benefit**—does the burden or expense of the proposed discovery outweigh its likely benefit, particularly in the case of the discovery of electronically stored information?

    3. Protective Orders—should the court limit the discoverability of the material through entry of a protective order?

B. ATTORNEY-CLIENT PRIVILEGE—is the material privileged from disclosure?

    1. Communication—does the material pertain to a communication?

    2. Confidentiality—did the communication occur in confidence exclusive of any third parties not party to the privileged relationship?

3. **Between an Attorney and Client**—was the communication between an attorney acting as such and her client?

4. **Legal Advice**—was the communication for the purpose of giving or seeking legal advice?

5. **Waiver**—was the privilege waived by disclosure of the communication to third parties outside of the privileged relationship?

C. **Work-Product Protection**—is the material protected from discovery by the work-product doctrine?

1. **Legal Thoughts**—does the material contain the mental impressions, conclusions, opinions, or legal theories of a representative of the party?

2. **Trial Preparation**—were the materials prepared in anticipation of litigation?

3. **Preparer of Material**—was the material prepared by or for the party receiving the request or by or for that party's representative?

4. **Substantial Need**—can the party requesting the material demonstrate they have a substantial need for the materials to prepare their case?

5. **Other Means**—can the party requesting the material demonstrate that they are unable without undue hardship to obtain the substantial equivalent of the materials by some other means?

PRE-ANSWER & DISPOSITIVE MOTIONS

A. ABILITY TO RAISE THE DEFENSE—can the defense be raised at this time?

1. **Nature of Defense**—does the defense claim a lack of personal jurisdiction, improper venue, ineffective process, or ineffective service of process (the waivable defenses)?

   a. If not, the defense may be raised at any time through trial. A challenge to subject matter jurisdiction may be raised at any time.

   b. If so, proceed to the next question.

2. **Timing of Motion**—if one of the waivable defenses is being raised, has any other defense, objection or responsive pleading already been submitted to the court? If not, it may be raised and must be consolidated with other waivable defenses the party intends to make.

B. VALIDITY OF THE DEFENSE (FAILURE TO STATE A CLAIM)—should the motion to dismiss for failure to state a claim be granted?

1. **Factual Challenge?** Does the motion challenge the factual allegations of the complaint? If so, the motion is not properly a motion to dismiss for failure to state a claim and may not be granted. If not, proceed to the next question.

2. **Legal Challenges?** If the motion challenges the legal sufficiency of the complaint, does the complaint, assuming the allegations to be true, entitle the claimant to relief under the applicable substantive law? If not, the complaint fails to state a claim and should be dismissed. Courts may also dismiss the complaint for failure to state a claim if it lacks factual allegations substantiating the legal claims asserted in the complaint.

C. SUMMARY JUDGMENT—should the court enter summary judgment?

1. **Movant's Party Status**—is the movant the party bearing the burden of proof on the claim at trial?

a. If so, the movant must identify or present the court with sufficient factual evidence to support its claim.

b. If not, then this burden falls on the non movant. The movant's burden of production may be satisfied simply by pointing to the record and indicating the absence of evidentiary support for the nonmovant's claim.

2. **Discharging the Plaintiff's Burden of Proof**—has the party bearing the burden of proof satisfied that burden?

a. **Admissible Evidence**—has the party carrying the burden of proof supported its claim with admissible factual evidence?

b. **Persuasive Evidence**—is the party's evidence persuasive or does the party's evidence disprove alternate reasonable explanations regarding the defendant's challenged conduct?

c. **Evidentiary Standard**—does the party's evidence prove its case to the degree required under the relevant evidentiary standard that would be applicable at trial?

JUDGMENT AS A MATTER OF LAW
& MOTION FOR NEW TRIAL

A. JUDGMENT AS A MATTER OF LAW—should the court enter judgment as a matter of law?

1. **Timing**—may judgment as a matter of law be entered at this time?

   a. Only proper if the party opposing judgment as a matter of law has completed the presentation of its evidence, and either

   b. The case has not been submitted to the jury, or

   c. The jury has issued a verdict and a prior motion for judgment as a matter of law is now being renewed.

2. **Evidentiary Support?** Is the nonmovant's case supported by sufficient evidence such that a reasonable jury could find in favor of that party?

   a. **No Evidence?** Has the nonmovant failed to present evidence establishing an essential element of its claim?

   b. **Substantial Evidence?** Do the facts and permissible inferences point overwhelmingly in favor of one party, such that reasonable people could not arrive at a contrary verdict?

B. NEW TRIAL—should a new trial be ordered?

1. **Time Limit**—have 10 days passed since judgment was entered in the case? If so, no new trial may be ordered.

2. **Grounds**—are there grounds for ordering a new trial?

   a. **Legal Errors**—has a reversible legal error occurred?

   b. **Erroneous Jury Verdict**—does the jury verdict go against the great weight of the evidence?

   c. **Excessive Verdict**—is the verdict grossly excessive such that it "shocks the conscience"? If so, the court may use *remittitur* to lower the awarded amount, forcing the plaintiff to accept the lower amount or face an order for a new trial.

d. **New Evidence**—has new evidence been discovered?

 i. If so, could the evidence have been discovered earlier through the exercise of due diligence?

 ii. If not, is the evidence material, in that it is likely to have an impact on the verdict?

e. **Improper Jury Influence**—has the jury been improperly influenced in such a way as to undermine faith in the verdict as the product of impartial decision making based only on the evidence presented at trial?

PRECLUSION DOCTRINE

A. CLAIM PRECLUSION—is the claim barred by a prior adjudication?

   1. Same Claim? Is the current claim the same as a claim raised in the prior action?

      a. **Identical Claims**—are the claims exactly identical?

      b. **Transactionally Related Claims**—do the claims arise out of the same transaction or series of connected transactions?

   2. Same Parties? Does the current action involve the same parties that were party to and adversaries in the original action?

      a. **Identical Parties**—are the parties in both actions identical?

      b. **Parties in Privity**—if a party in the current action was not a party to the original action, is there a relationship between that party and a party in the original action that warrants treating the non-party to the initial action as if it were a party?

   3. Final Judgment? Was the prior action concluded by a final judgment on the merits?

      a. **Judgments for Plaintiff**—if the prior case was resolved in favor of the plaintiff, it is considered a final judgment on the merits.

      b. **Judgments for Defendant**—if the case was resolved in favor of the defendant, the resolution is not treated as a final judgment on the merits if it was dismissed for lack of jurisdiction, improper venue, or failure to join a party under Rule 19. Otherwise, a resolution for a defendant is considered a final judgment on the merits unless otherwise indicated.

B. ISSUE PRECLUSION—has an issue already been conclusively resolved between the parties in a prior action?

1. **Same Parties?** Does the current action involve the same parties that were parties to and adversaries in the original action? See Part A.2 above for the steps in this analysis. Remember that it is possible for one who was not a party to the prior action to invoke issue preclusion against an adversary in a subsequent action based on the fact that the adversary fully litigated and lost that issue previously (nonmutual collateral estoppel).

2. **Same Issue?** Is the issue raised in the prior action identical in all respects to the issue raised in the current action?

3. **Actually Litigated and Determined?** Was the issue actually litigated and determined in the prior action, meaning the issue was raised and argued by the parties?

4. **Necessary to the Judgment?** Was resolution of the issue in question necessary to the judgment reached in the case?

   a. **Outcome Determinative**—would a different decision regarding the issue have affected the outcome of the case?

   b. **Multiple Grounds**—is it unclear on which of multiple grounds for relief a judgments relies?

†